# SPORTING
# COLLECTIBLES

## Jim and Vivian Karsnitz

1469 Morstein Road, West Chester, Pennsylvania 19380

*Dedicated*
*To*
JIM & BARB
CRAIG & KATHI
PATRICK, MICHAEL, ROSS AND TRISTAN

Published by Schiffer Publishing, Ltd.
1469 Morstein Road
West Chester, Pennsylvania 19380
Please write for a free catalog.
This book may be purchased from the publisher.
Please include $2.00 postage.
Try your bookstore first.

We are interested in hearing from authors
with book ideas on related subjects.

Title page:
Yellowlegs in the Audubon Position *****
made by the Ward brothers

Copyright © 1992 by Jim and Vivian Karsnitz.
Library of Congress Catalog Number: 91-67009.

Printed in the United States of America.
ISBN: 0-88740-385-9

## Acknowledgements

We would like to thank all of our friends who
encouraged us to write this book and also the
many new friends we made while gathering
our material. Please keep the information
coming.

We give special thanks to the following
people who gave us abundant help: Robert
Coleman, Art and Fay Gutshall, Robert Litzen-
berg, J. Evans McKinney, Michael Murphy,
Harold A. Reist, Donald Rhoads, Lisa and Ken
Trayer, Robert P. Shaffer and William
Wagenhurst.

# Contents

Foreword . . . . . . . . . . . . . . . . . . . . . . . . . . . . . . . . . . . . . . . . 4
Chapter 1    About Sporting Antiques . . . . . . . . . . . . . . . . . . . . . . . 5
Chapter 2    Decoys . . . . . . . . . . . . . . . . . . . . . . . . . . . . . . . . . . . . . . 10
           *Working Decoys* . . . . . . . . . . . . . . . . . . . . . . . . . . . . . 10
           *Factory Decoys* . . . . . . . . . . . . . . . . . . . . . . . . . . . . . . 27
           *Decorative Decoys* . . . . . . . . . . . . . . . . . . . . . . . . . . 40
           *Shorebirds and Songbirds* . . . . . . . . . . . . . . . . . . . 44
           *Miniatures* . . . . . . . . . . . . . . . . . . . . . . . . . . . . . . . . . 50
Chapter 3    Hand Loading Tools and Supplies . . . . . . . . . . . . . . . 56
Chapter 4    Shot Shell Boxes and Shells . . . . . . . . . . . . . . . . . . . 61
Chapter 5    Target Balls . . . . . . . . . . . . . . . . . . . . . . . . . . . . . . . . 79
Chapter 6    Licenses . . . . . . . . . . . . . . . . . . . . . . . . . . . . . . . . . . . 85
Chapter 7    Traps . . . . . . . . . . . . . . . . . . . . . . . . . . . . . . . . . . . . . . 88
Chapter 8    Sporting Books . . . . . . . . . . . . . . . . . . . . . . . . . . . . . 98
Chapter 9    Paper Arts . . . . . . . . . . . . . . . . . . . . . . . . . . . . . . . . . 100
Chapter 10   Sporting Prints . . . . . . . . . . . . . . . . . . . . . . . . . . . . . 111
Chapter 11   Advertisements . . . . . . . . . . . . . . . . . . . . . . . . . . . . . 117
Chapter 12   Hanging Game Pictures . . . . . . . . . . . . . . . . . . . . . . 128
Chapter 13   Glassware and China . . . . . . . . . . . . . . . . . . . . . . . . 130
Chapter 14   Stamps . . . . . . . . . . . . . . 143
Chapter 15   Accessories . . . . . . . . . 147
           Bibliography . . . . . . . . 158
           Index . . . . . . . . . . . . . . 159

Pneumatic Great Horned Owl \*\*\*\*
Complete Set made by the Hoosier Call and
Decoy Company of Delphi, Indiana. *Courtesy of
Brickerville Antiques and Decoys*

# Foreword

The writers have been collecting items concerned with the outdoors for over forty years. We started with decoys, but soon discovered many other related items. In our attempt to learn more about each one, we found good books on decoys, guns and some prints and advertisements, but little or nothing on most of the other fields. Over the years we have picked up bits of information from other collectors, dealers, museums and the people who actually used the items in their pursuits.

This book reflects our experiences. It is not intended as a comprehensive list of everything in the field, but rather a survey of the items available. We have concentrated on lesser-known collectibles. Our hope is to shed light on the unusual and to inspire people to enjoy them.

*Ward Brothers Decoys* ***
Milton C. Weiler, 1971
23 by 17 inches

# CHAPTER 1

# *About Sporting Antiques*

In writing about sporting antiques, it is necessary first to define our subject. Sporting can be interpreted many ways, but we have chosen items concerned with hunting, fishing and wildlife in general. Of interest are items used in taking fish, birds and animals primarily, but also the literature, pictures and objects common to people who love nature.

By strict definition, an "antique" must be one hundred years old. We do not adhere strictly to this interpretation, but consider anything no longer manufactured as a collectible. Some include as collectibles newer items that are a continuation of antiques such as reprints of books and prints or reissues of objects such as the Remington bullet knives. Whatever pleases you is fair game. As the book unfolds, you will discover that both the common and rare are interesting. You need not be a practicing hunter or an avid angler to collect the items.

You need only to love nature and the objects associated with it. There is a great diversity of sporting items, enough variety to satisfy the active and the passive collector alike. Pursuit of the activity requires only imagination and persistence. The enjoyment can be either in the field or in the armchair.

Some may feel that by collecting sporting items one tacitly approves of the use of guns in killing. While this attitude may be shared by some collectors, it is not the attitude of all. A sense of history, the romance of earlier times, and appreciation of early craftsmanship also lead to collecting these items. A serious collector who studies and researches his collection usually becomes a conservationist; preserving the artifacts and understanding their use often leads to an appreciation of the necessity for conservation.

Once you are drawn to collecting sporting

Marble Arms Co., Gladstone,
  Michigan ★★★★
with 10-inch blade, 14¾ inches long,
Remington Bullet Knife #R4243
Remington Fish Knife #R1513
Remington Bullet Knife #1306
Marbles Trout Knife
*Eugene Showaker Collection*

5

Target ball display

items, the question of what to concentrate on arises. A person hardly ever sits down and makes a rational decision about what they will collect. Usually, the interest evolves over a period of time by exposure to other collections, what may come your way, or be inherited from someone in your family. Fond memories of past experiences or a technical interest in some phase of sport may also move you in a certain direction.

Some people rationalize their collecting by referring to it primarily as an investment. This may prove unwise. While you may become lucky and have your collection increase in value, you probably will enjoy it far more if you acquire what you like rather than what you think will provide for your retirement. Investments should be made in areas readily convertible into cash. With collectibles, usually some time is required to find a person willing and able to pay the best price. If you still feel you need your collection to increase in value, buy only the best condition and concentrate on rarer items. Actually this advice holds true even if investment value is of minimum concern and it applies the same for any antique or collectible.

A "collector" can be one who picks up items as they become available in passing or one who pursues his interest at every opportunity. Some people are what we call "accumulators"; they get items and lay them aside. For them the pursuit is the thrill and quantity is more important than knowledge. Others set definite goals such as completing a set of some sort and displaying it. Some people have a space that needs filling and will buy only what conforms to their decor. Other collectors eventually become "antique dealers" who sell surplus items that they have replaced by upgrading their collection. They also want to make contacts to purchase additional items and thus add to their collections. In collecting, there is no substitute for knowledge. The one who knows his field will acquire what others miss and avoid repaired or reproduced items. If your knowledge is limited or growing, give your trust and your questions to a reputable dealer.

The process of finding additions to your collection can lead you to many unusual places. It is trite, but true, to say that "they are where you find them". There is no one place to hunt. Rather, there are many, from the obvious antique shops and shows, flea markets and auctions to gun shows, magazine advertisements, friends and collectors associations. A true benefit of the hunt is the companionship of many wonderful people you meet on the collecting road. Some will become good friends and others will expand your horizons by leading you down different avenues. It becomes more fun when friends and spouses team up for the hunt. Perhaps one partner searches for guns and the other the shells and advertisements to complement the guns, or one hunts for decoys and the other books on wildfowl-related subjects. Involving your children by allowing them to collect what they want makes it a family activity.

This book concentrates on American-made items even though there are countless

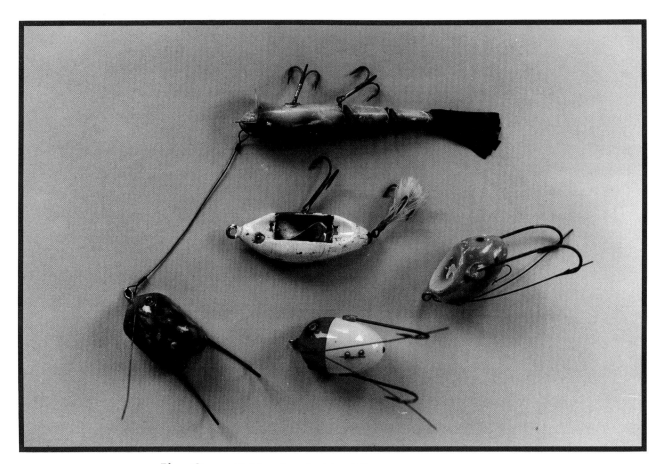

Plug-Oreno #959 red and white \*\*\*
Plug-Oreno #959 Frog Finish \*\*\*
by South Bend Bait Co., South Bend, Indiana Muskie
Minnow in three hinged sections \*\*\*\*
by Erwin Weller Co., Sioux City, Iowa Creek Chub
Weed Bug, frog finish \*\*\*
Chippewa Bass Bait \*\*\*
*Jeff Rudy collection*

possibilities from other countries as well. The opportunities are endless, limited only by your imagination. And your collecting can be fitted to your wallet as well as your taste, for scarce items can be inexpensive, too.

Preservation and maintenance of your treasurers is also important. Humidity or lack of it, rust or improper storage can damage or even destroy your hard won pieces. Use of inappropriate preservation methods or materials can also cause damage. It is important to experiment and work slowly at first before preceding with any preservation. Consulting with other collectors or professional restorers is very helpful and if the item is valuable consider using the services of a professional. As a general rule the less done the better and the goal is to keep it as close to its original condition as possible.

Keeping your collection in the home where you and others can enjoy it is probably the main goal. While you cannot duplicate museum conditions you can control humidity to some extent and provide appropriate display conditions. Covered cases for fragile items and coverings or stands for others will do this. Old working decoys can have a good grade of paste wax applied and then hand buffed. This preserves the finish and makes cleaning easier, but do not do this to decorative ones. They may be too fragile and the wax may build up in the feathering detail.

Handling things in your collection while showing it or looking at others rare items, can be a problem. Clean, dry hands are necessary when holding paper, metal or glass. A pet peeve is anyone picking up decoys by the neck and head. Using the head as a handle can

7

seriously damage an old decoy. While looking at a dealers stock, handle carefully, it must be presented to another customer if you don't buy it.

Framing paper material using museum mounting is best, but you can also preserve it by having it placed on foam board and shrink drying a clear plastic over it. Paper shot shell boxes can be wrapped in plastic and other items can be placed in specialized albums like stamps, postcards, envelopes or tokens. Rust should be removed if possible, but at least a rust inhibitor like "WD-40" should be applied. Remember, the goal is to stay as close to original condition as practical.

The display of a collection is as individual as each collector. Do you want your collection to be the focal point of your office or home? Many people do, and therefore use furniture and accessaries to accomplish this. Do you want your collection in one room or scattered throughout the place? Your imagination is your only limit. Suit yourself and you will please others.

Lighting may play an important part of your display. Consider the possibilities. Track lighting, spot lights or a lit case can highlight the pieces. A new bulb with glare free pure white light is now available.

Colors used could bring out certain aspects of your collection. Let your imagination run wild. If you use a professional interior decorator to help accomplish what you want, be sure to communicate your ideas clearly.

The security of your collection should be considered when planning the display. Perhaps a professional should be consulted. It is important to maintain an inventory with a description and a photograph or a video picture, the initial cost as well as the current value. The value should be verified by an appraiser recognized by your insurance company. If you have a computer, the inventory is easily set up on a data base, with many options. It is especially important for a gun collection to be inventoried with the serial numbers included. When you have adequately secured your collection, you can be more relaxed to enjoy it—And isn't that a big reason to collect?

Peters boxes, similar design ***

## VALUES

The subject of value can be very controversial. Things like condition, desirability, size, fashion, number available and economic conditions all combine to set the price. Some of these are subjective evaluations and all are subject to change. One professional hardly ever agrees with another in all cases and auction prices may reflect the heat of the battle rather than rational decisions. In view of this we have not attempted a price guide, but have settled on a rarity rating. We will use five stars to rate rarity as follows:

\* Common, readily available.
\*\* Not plentiful, but can be found by searching.
\*\*\* Rare, may take some time to find.
\*\*\*\* Very rare, difficult to find.
\*\*\*\*\* Special or one of a kind.

Good Hunting!

Owl and Pussy Cat covered cheese dish \*\*\*\*          Base of the Owl and Pussy Cat dish

# CHAPTER 2

# *Decoys*

Many good books have been written about decoys so this text will be held to a minimum. Decoys are of special interest to sporting collectors and they are classified here in four categories; working decoys, decorative decoys, shorebirds and songbirds and miniature decoys.

## WORKING DECOYS

Working decoys are those replicas of birds made to be used while hunting, usually ducks and geese. They were either handcrafted or factory-made.

Each geographic area where hunting took place has had many decoy carvers. These areas include all the migratory flyways and many regional territories. Locally handcrafted decoys have become part of the history and folk art from each area.

Pair of Redheads ***
made by the Ward brothers

Pair of 1936 Canvasbacks ***
made by the Ward brothers of
Crisfield, Maryland

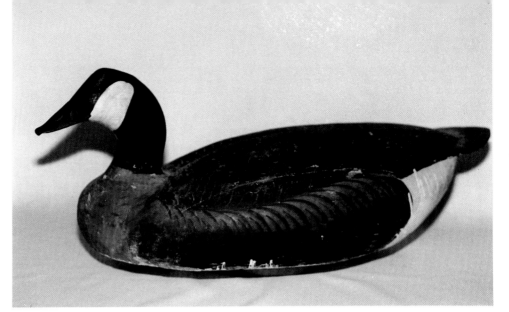

Canada Goose \*\*\*
made by the Ward brothers

Pair of Ruddy Ducks \*\*\*
made by the Ward brothers

Oversize Drake Canvasback \*\*\*
made by the Ward brothers

Experimental Drake Canvasback
made by Steve Ward

Drake Goldeneye Decoy
made by the Ward brothers for the
author in 1967

MADE BY STEVE
PAINTED LEM
WARD BRO.
CRISFIELD, MD
1936
(Lem Ward) MODEL Steve Ward
1967 SHOOTING -1967-
STOOL

To Jim and Vivian
With Love

The Ward brothers in their...

Drake Shoveler **
carved by Norris Pratt and painted by Lem
Ward

Canada Goose ***
made by Capt. Ike Langford of Crisfield, Maryland, a
maker of punt guns

Hen Merganser ***
made by Ira Hudson of Chincoteague, Virginia

Hen Merganser ***
made by Miles Hancock of Chincoteague, Virginia

Drake Merganser ***
made by Ira Hudson of Chincoteague, Virginia

Drake Canvasback **
made by James "Corb" Reed of Chincoteague, Virginia.
Note the feet carved in the body.

Black Duck **
made by Delbert "Cigar" Daisey of Chincoteague, Virginia

Cigar Daisey's signature

Brant ****
made by Nathan Cobb
of Cobb Island, Virginia

Pair of Canvasbacks **
made by Capt. Josh Traver of Vienna, Maryland

Canada Goose ***
made by Edward J. Phillips of Cambridge,
Maryland

Brant **
made by Charlie Joiner of Chestertown,
Maryland

Canada Goose **
made by Horace Graham of
Charlestown, Maryland.

Pair of Canvasback sleepers **
made by Charlie Joiner of Chestertown, Maryland

Pair of Canvasbacks **
made by Will Heverin of Charlestown, Maryland

Pair Canvasbacks **
made by Sam Barnes of Havre de Grace,
Maryland

Drake Canvasback sleeper ***
made by Jim Currier of Havre de Grace,
Maryland

Canada Goose **
Made by Jim Pierce of Havre de Grace,
Maryland

Pair of Blue Bills **
made by Bob Litzenberg of Elkton, Maryland

Swan ***
made by Jim Pierce of Havre de Grace, Maryland

Pair of Pintails ***
made by Bob Litzenberg of Elkton, Maryland

Sink Box Decoys **
one iron, one wooden

Pair of Buffleheads *
made from cork net floats

Swan ***
made by Norris Pratt of
Kemblesville, Pennsylvania

Susquehanna River Drake Canvasback **
made by Walt Eveler of Brogue, Pennsylvania

Susquehanna River Drake Canvasback **
made by Ralph Gipe of Craley, Pennsylvania

Susquehanna River canvas covered Canada
Goose ***
made by Ralph Gipe of Craley, Pennsylvania

Susquehanna River Drake
Canvasback sleeper ***
made by Robert Erwin of
Washington Boro, Pennsylvania

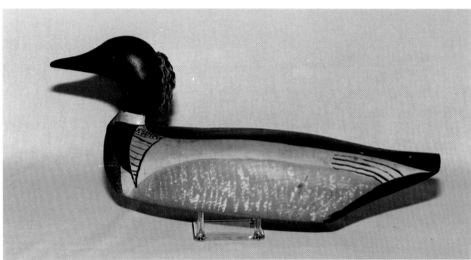

Maine Drake Merganser **
made with sisal head feathers

Full body Canada Goose field decoy *

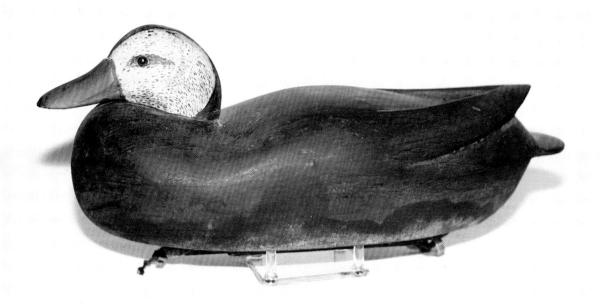

Delaware River Black Duck ***
made by Vincent Goddard of Roebling, New Jersey

Canvas flying Drake Mallard ***

Pair of Buffleheads **
made by Vic Berg of Kitty Hawk, North Carolina. Note the ship-like keel.

Y board *

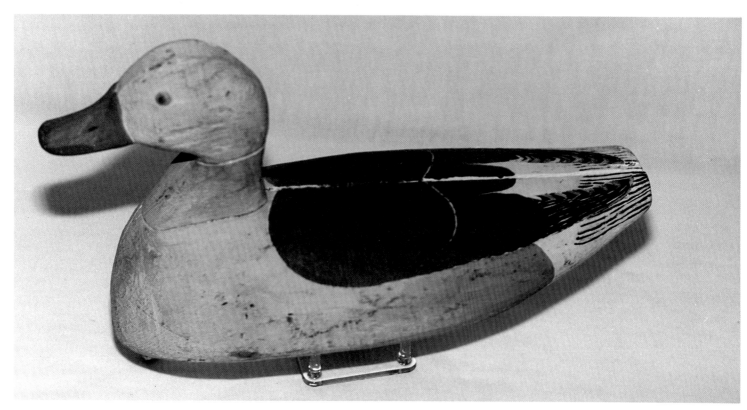

Sea Gull confidence decoy ***

Feeder decoys **

24

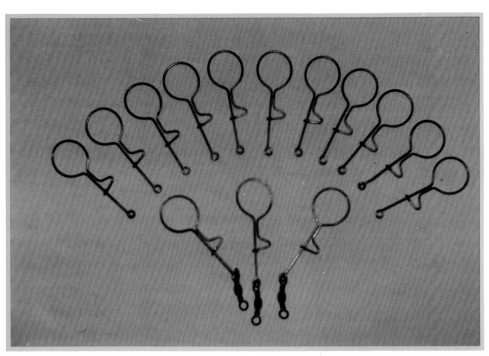

Live decoy leg holds **

Pratt keels ***

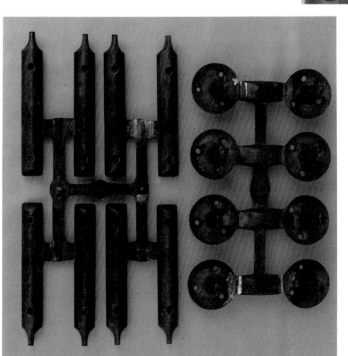

Pratt keel and anchor molds ***

Assorted decoy weights and keels *

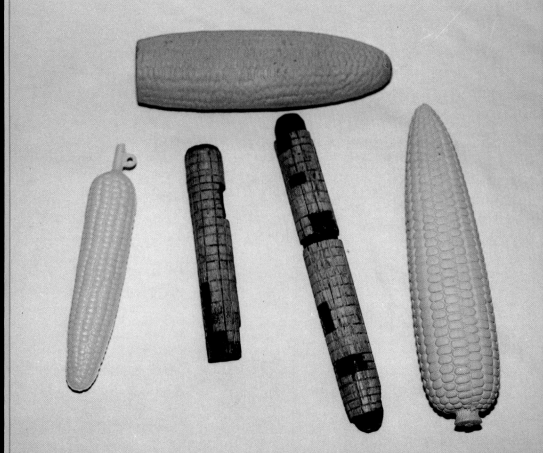

Decoy corn **

26

## FACTORY DECOYS

Factory decoys were made by many companies in a wide variety of materials. For example collectors enjoy searching for Animal Trap Co.(ATCO) decoys from Pennsylvania which might include miniatures, a real gem to find. Also, the companies Mason, Dodge, Stevens and Pratt are just a few of the many decoy producing companies which made birds from wood, cork, papier mache, hard and soft plastic, waxed cardboard, tin, wicker and canvas, and combinations of these materials.

If you can find a U.S. patent number on your decoy or in the literature, you can write the U.S. Patent Office in Washington, D.C. and for a nominal fee get a copy of the patent. This is true of any patented artifact.

Swan **
Made by the Herter Company of Waseca, Minnesota

Drake Eider **
made by the Herter Company of Waseca, Minnesota

Dupe-a-goose **
made by the Dunster Sporting Goods Company of Seattle, Washington. *Courtesy of Brickerville Antiques and Decoys.*

Drake Mallard ***
with a papier maché body made by the Flap-o-matic
Company of Chicago, Illinois

Pair of Mallards ***
with plastic bodies made by the Flap-o-matic Company
*Courtesy of Brickerville Antiques and Decoys*

Patent paper Flap-o-matic, Frank J.
Benedetto, inventor

Pair of stuffed mallards ****
made by Decoys DeLux of Morrison, Illinois *Courtesy of
Brickerville Antiques and Decoys*

Pair of Mallards ****
made by Airtite of Danville, Illinois *Courtesy of Brickerville
Antiques and Decoys*

Black Duck ***
made by Fibro-Lite Products Company of
Minneapolis, Minnesota *Courtesy of Brickerville
Antiques and Decoys*

Drake Mallard ***
made by The Rose Folding
Decoy Company of Chicago,
Illinois *Courtesy of Brickerville
Antiques and Decoys*

Wooden box ***
from the Canvas Decoy
Company of Union City,
Tennessee *Courtesy of Brickerville Antiques and Decoys*

Pair of Mallards **
Folding canvas decoys made by
J.W. Reynolds Co. in Chicago,
Illinois *Courtesy of Brickerville
Antiques and Decoys*

Hen Mallard ****
an Acme Folding Decoy made by the St. Louis Brass
Manufacturing Company of St. Louis Manufacturing Company of St. Louis, Missouri. *Courtesy of
Brickerville Antiques and Decoys*

Dove ***
made by the Brooks Company of Houston, Texas
*Courtesy of Brickerville Antiques and Decoys*

Drake Mallard ***
made by the Balsa King Decoy Company of Belmont,
California *Courtesy of Brickerville Antiques and Decoys*

Drake Pintail ***
with a cork body, canvas head, and wire and canvas tail
made by the Scott Cork Decoy Company of Oakland,
California *Courtesy of Brickerville Antiques and Decoys*

Deweys Owl and Crow Decoy Complete Set ****
made by the Outing Manufacturing Company of
Elkhart, Indiana *Courtesy of Brickerville Antiques and Decoys*

Pair of Pintails **
made by the William R. Johnson Company of Seattle,
Washington *Courtesy of Brickerville Antiques and Decoys*

Pair of Mallard field decoys **
made by the William R. Johnson Company of Seattle,
Washington *Courtesy of Brickerville Antiques and Decoys*

Pair of Golden Eyes
with canvas bodies and wooden heads made by the
Herters Company of Waseca, Minnesota. *Courtesy of
Binkerville Antiques and Decoys*

Pair of Mallards
K-D Decoy (Knocked Down) made by
the Specialty Manufacturing Company
of St. Paul, Minnesota

Pair Mallard feeders
made by Wildfowler Decoys of Old
Saybrook, Connecticut.

34

Wicker Canada Goose **

Oversize Pintails **
Victor Decoys made by the
Animal Trap Company of
Pascagoula, Mississippi

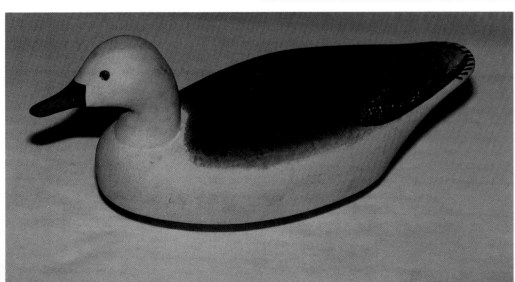

Seagull confidence decoy **
made by Wildfowler Decoys of
Point Pleasant, New Jersey

Drake Bluebill **
made by the Animal Trap Company of Pascagoula,
Mississippi

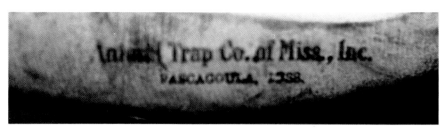

Animal Trap Company (ATCO) logo

Dove Tree **

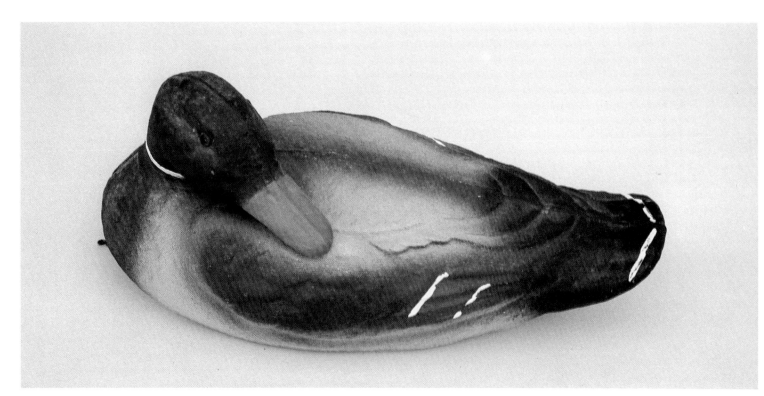

Drake Mallard sleeper ***
Victor Decoys made by the Animal Trap Company

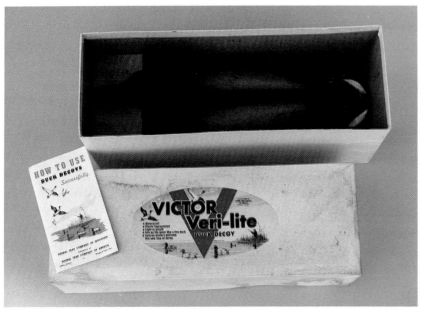

Drake Mallard ***
which was sent as a sample to customers by the Animal Trap Company

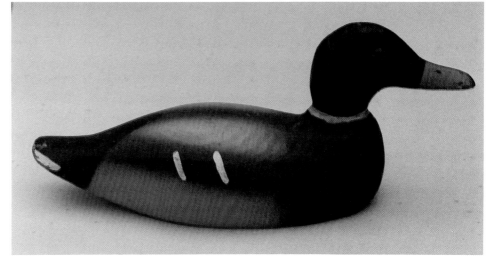

Drake Mallard ***
a sanded, Victor First Grade decoy made by the Animal Trap Company

Owls **

37

Victor Owl and Crows **

Crow **
made by an unknown factory

Cloth Crow and Owl ***
filled with chicken feathers and made by the Boyd
Martin Decoy Company of Delphi, Indiana

Crows *

## DECORATIVE DECOYS

Decorative decoys are birds hand carved and painted in life-like homage to nature which are used for interior decoration; they never see the water.

Among prominent "fathers" of the decorative birds were the brothers Lem (1896-1984) and Steve (1895-1976) Ward from Crisfield, Maryland. They helped to evolve working decoys into decorative birds. Many years ago we visited the Crab Derby in Crisfield where a small decoy show was held in a shed over the water at the end of Main Street. Here we met the Ward Brothers who spent a great deal of time with us and our two boys and we remained friends for the rest of their lives. The Wards were masters of carving birds in many natural positions beyond the turned heads commonly seen before they started their innovations. Even their working birds had slightly turned heads. From their start other decorative carvers began to experiment with poses and went on to further developments such as life-like feathering and including natural surroundings in the carvings. Many other decoy carvers now compete for prize money and satisfaction at large and small competitions.

Grouse ****
made by Oliver Lawson

Pair of Quail ****
made by Oliver Lawson of Crisfield, Maryland

Canada Goose, 1967 ****
made by the Ward Brothers

Drake Bufflehead **** made by John Cunningham of
Lebanon, Pennsylvania

Hen Pintail *****
with carved wooden natural surroundings made by
Oliver Lawson

Drake Bufflehead ****
made by Jim West of Bordentown, New Jersey

Drake Pintail ****
made by Decoys Unlimited of Erie, Pennsylvania

## SHOREBIRDS AND SONGBIRDS

Carvings of shorebirds and songbirds can be a field of collectibles all their own. Old shorebirds are extremely hard to find and it's sometimes difficult to identify the old from the new. The songbirds carved by contemporary artists can be found in a multitude of species and degree of sophistication, enough to satisfy any pocketbook.

As with the ducks and geese, these birds originally were made by individual carvers and factories as working birds as well as "decoratives". Collectors not especially interested in wildfowl might chose to concentrate on songbirds and raptors in their search for beauty and quality in the wide area of sporting art.

Tinnies **
made by Strater & Sohier of Boston, Massachusetts

Marbled Godwit ***
made by Robert Clifford of Brewster, Massachusetts

Mourning Dove ***
made by Madison Mitchell of Havre de Grace, Maryland

Flicker ****
made by Oliver Lawson

Black Bellied Plover \*\*\*\*
made by Bob Litzenberg of Elkton, Maryland *Courtesy of Brickerville Antiques and Decoy Shop*

Yellowlegs \*\*\*
made by J. Lloyd Sterling
of Crisfield, Maryland

Woodcock ***
made by J. Lloyd Sterling

Flicker decoy ***
made by J. Lloyd Sterling

Golden Plover ***
made by Miles Hancock of Chincoteague, Virginia

Black Bellied Plover ***
made by Miles Hancock of Chincoteague, Virginia

**Oyster catcher \*\*\***
made by Miles Hancock of Chincoteague, Virginia

**Curlew \*\*\***
made by Miles Hancock of Chincoteague, Virginia

**Shorebirds \*\*\***
by the Herters Company including the Black Bellied
Plover, Curlew, and Pigeon

Peep **
made by Lloyd Tyler, 4 inches

Yellowlegs ***
made by Miles Hancock of Chincoteague, Virginia

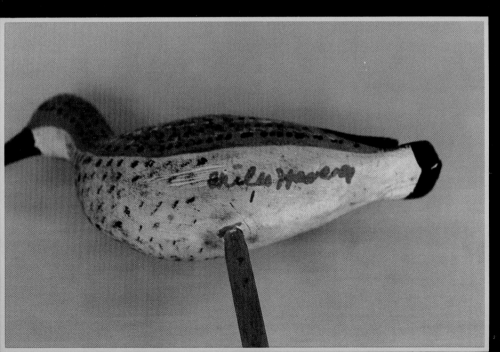

Signature on the Yellowlegs
by Miles Hancock

# MINIATURES

Many collectors, especially those with limited space, find it desirable to collect bird art made not in life-size but in miniature. Many of the famous decoy makers also made miniatures. They are a prize to find and have launched a whole sub-category in today's interests at shows and competitions. In the early years, Bob McGaw of Havre de Grace, MD (1879-1958) is known to have had a basket of miniatures which he peddled for $.50 apiece. Elmer Crowell, from East Harwich, MA (1862-1951) is one of the most famous carvers of miniature pairs. These could be purchased originally in sporting stores like Abercrombie & Fitch in New York City. Capt. Jesse Urie of Rock Hall, MD (1901-1978) was one of the Chesapeake Bay's most prolific miniature carvers. His miniature sets consisted of ten pairs which were exact duplicates of his regular size decoys. ATCO made miniatures to be used for their salesmen as samples, and some were given as gifts to their board members and good customers. Much later, the CarryLite Company made plastic miniatures, which are still a nice set to find. Many other early and recent miniatures can be found to tickle a collector's interest.

Brant ***
made by the Ward brothers, 9 inches

Logo of the Ward brothers

Canada Goose ***
made by the Ward brothers, 9½ inches

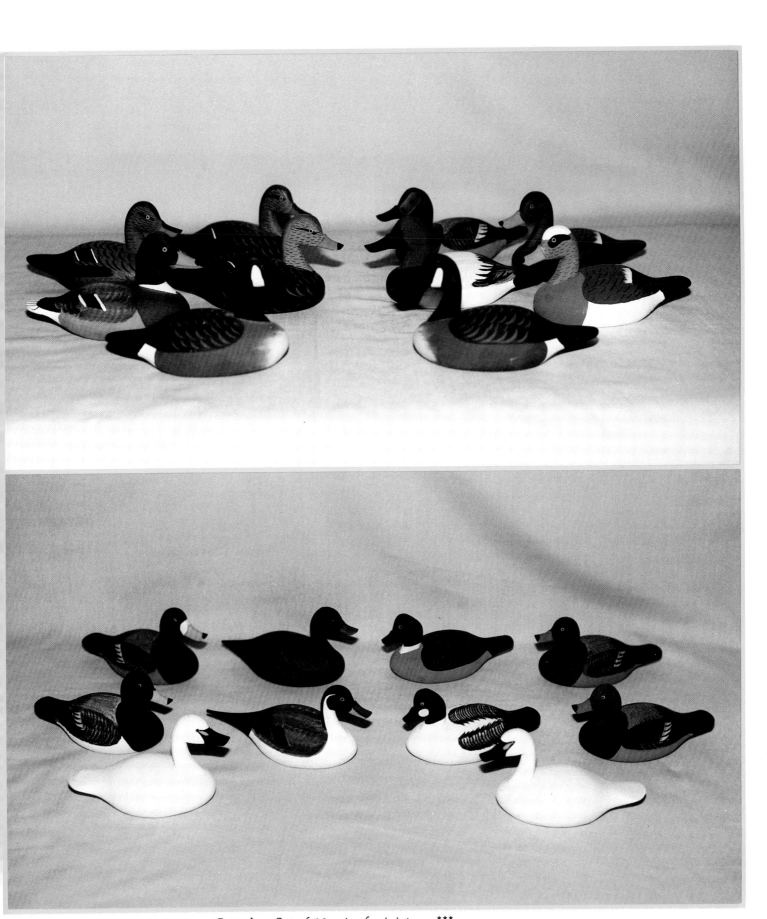

Complete Set of 10 pair of miniatures***
made by Capt. Jesse Urie of Rock Hall, Maryland, 5¾
inches

Pair of Canvasbacks***
made by Jim Pierce, 8½ inches

Pair of Pintails***
made by Jim Pierce, 9½ inches

Mallard (6½ inches) and Widgeon pair (5½ inches) ***
made by J. Lloyd Sterling

Victor decoy ***
made by the Animal Trap Company of Lititz,
Pennsylvania, 7 inches

Logo of the Victor decoys

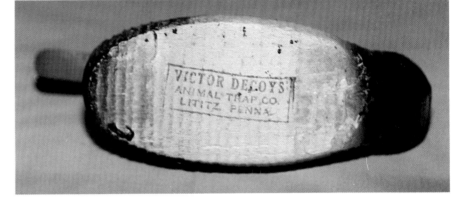

Canada Goose ***
made by Oliver Lawson, 8¼ inches

Canada Goose ***
made by Miles Hancock

Logo of Miles Hancock

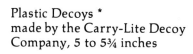

Papier Maché decoys **
4¾ to 7 inches

Plastic Decoys *
made by the Carry-Lite Decoy
Company, 5 to 5¾ inches

54

Pair of Canvasbacks and Bluebill ****
made by Scott Jackson before 1926 in Charlestown,
Maryland

Swan, Goose, and Hen Canvasback ***
made by Bob McGaw in 1930

# CHAPTER 3

# Hand Loading Tools and Supplies

The supplies and tools needed to load and reload shells for shotguns provide the individual with great collecting opportunities. Many sportsmen loaded their own ammunition, either because they wanted to control the amount of powder and shot they used to their own preferences, or because they saved money by doing it themselves.

Hunters would purchase their gun loading supplies in quantity; shot shells, powder, shot, primers and wads. Shot shells could be purchased with the primer already in the shell or not, and the primer could be removed from used shot shells and a new one inserted. Brass shells were also reloaded and were worth the extra expense over paper shells because of the many times they could be reused. The brass was not affected by dampness as were the paper shells.

Once the hunter had assembled his supplies, he needed the specific tools to accomplish the task. A different set of reloading tools was needed for each gauge of shell. The process goes like this: first, he had to remove the old primer. This was done by driving a nail in the end of the de-capper against the primer on the inside of the used shell. The new primer was seated by using the re-capper. Next the shells were sometimes placed in a wooden block to keep them steady while the powder, shot and wads were added. The loader, a funnel type device, was slipped over the open shell and it was now ready to receive the powder and shot. The measure was used to determine the correct amount of powder to use and the powder was poured into the shell. Next, a felt wad was tamped down into the shell by the wadder, and over this was poured shot, also from the

Eureka shot shell loading set **
20 gauge

measure. Several more felt wads were then tamped down before a cardboard wad was finally put in place. The shells were then removed from the wooden block and placed into a crimper clamped to a table. The handle of the crimper was turned while the arm was pressed against the head. This pressure and the turning of the crimper rolled the end of the paper and formed the crimp. With brass shells, there could be no crimping so often a drop of tallow or wax was dropped on the top wad, waterproofing and sealing the round.

From this loading process come many collectibles. The realm of shot shells is fertile territory for different types of shells and the myriad number of head stamps. A collection could be formed with different sizes of shells from the large 2 gauge to the tiny 9 millimeter or a collection of brass shells. Shells can be found in 9 millimeter, and gauges of 410, 32, 28, 24, 20, 16, 14, 12, 10, 8, 4, 3, 2, and the yacht shells at 2½ gauge. The 12 gauge is by far the most common, and we even have a 13 gauge shell.

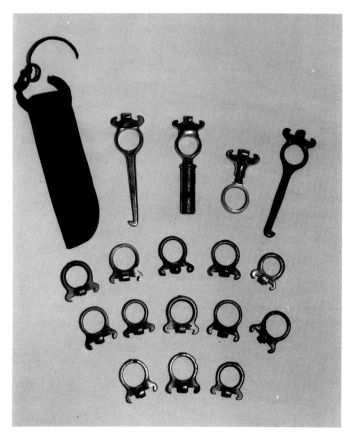

Extractor rings **
Some with attached whistles or tools

Reloading set and supplies **

Other major areas for collectibles today are the tools used in reloading. They were sold in sets and are found in all gauges. Some were very utilitarian, to be economical, while others are of higher quality using rosewood and brass in their components. English tools are especially fancy. It is quite a challenge to assemble a set in every gauge available.

An additional tool some re-loaders used was a wad cutter. This tool cut wads from pieces of felt or cardboard and saved the cost of buying wads.

An especially interesting tool in the set was the extractor ring. This was not used in reloading. Before the days of the automatic ejector, a shooter needed a tool to remove stuck cartridges from the gun. He wore an extractor ring on his finger for this purpose.

There were many variations made of these tools as companies vied with each other with their own "improvements". It is fascinating to see how many special labor-saving devices you can find.

Powder cans are a great potential for collectibles. They are made from tin or similar metal. Many are flat, like tobacco tins, and held a half to one pound of powder. The larger tins were round and held five or more pounds. The colorful labels attract attention. Many companies had their own ideas of what a label should look like. One California company made "Gold Dust" powder that is colored yellow rather than the regular grey-black. The DuPont Company made a series of labels with a specific number of "F"s on the label designating the fineness of the grind, and they are collectible. They started with one "F" and went to four (FFFF), the finest. When more than one "F" is on the label, the design looks much like a series of "H"s. Do not be misled, it is still a series of "F"s. Over the years, The DuPont Company bought up most of the rival powder companies: today, they no longer make powder.

There is some question about how safe powder cans are if they still contain powder. Black powder is a mixture of potassium nitrate, charcoal and sulphur and will not deteriorate unless moisture gets into it. When this happens it will corrode the can. It has a low ignition point and is not subject to spontaneous combustion. Smokeless powder is nitrated hydrocarbons plus additives depending on its

Three powder cans **
from the DuPont Powder Company
See detail next page.

Powder cans **
by the Robin Hood Powder
Company, Laflin & Rand
Company, and King's Powder
Company

58

Back of the DuPont powder can.
Shown on the previous page.

Powder can \*\*\*\*
by the Economy Powder Company of Reading,
Pennsylvania

use. Both powders are not, of themselves, a problem if left alone; but the prudent collector will empty the cans before displaying them. A fire in the home could be made more disastrous because of the powder, and moisture could destroy black powder cans. In the case of "gold dust" powder, you might want to use a baby food jar to display the powder along with the can.

Shot bags are also collectible, although not too plentiful. The old linen bags are the most desirable. Many cities had shot towers and each printed its name and logo on the bag. The usual size is the 25 pound bag, but there are some as small as five pounds. The city of Baltimore, Maryland has a shot tower still standing which can be seen from the popular Inner Harbor area. It looks like a brick smokestack. Molten lead was dropped through a screen at the top and landed in water at the bottom. The size of the screen determined the shot size. The lead became round droplets as it fell and cooled in the water.

Powder cans ** (above)
Snap Shot, by Canadian Industries, Montreal; DuPont; and Quickshot by King Powder Company, Cincinnati.

Powder cans ** (below)
by the American Powder Company, Oakland, NJ, Gold Dust by U.S. Powder Company of San Francisco, California; and Kings Powder Company, Cincinnati, Ohio

# CHAPTER 4

# Shot Shell Boxes and Shells

The shot shell boxes holding 25 shells are a colorful lot. Each manufacturer's art work was designed to appeal to the buyer. Pictures of game, dogs and hunters in various action poses adorned the boxes. The earlier boxes were made in two pieces, the tops fitting over the bottoms. Later, boxes were made from one piece of folded cardboard. The earlier examples are more desirable, but one piece boxes are also eagerly collected. True shot shell collectors gather all the boxes they can, making distinctions between the same designs that have different printing. Many collectors are satisfied with one of each design, but some pursue the almost impossible goal of getting one of each type made.

Another kind of box was made to hold 100 "new primed empty" (NPE) shells which were used by re-loaders. Most boxes are rather drab, but a series known as "Christmas Boxes" is eagerly sought after. They are named so because of the colorful red, white and blue colors and the wonderful pictures on them. They are extremely scarce and expensive.

In the late 1920s, Remington Arms Company produced the Remington Game Loads. These were specific loads with specific size shot for game pictured on the box. The game included Goose, Grouse, Snipe, Heavy Duck, Rabbit, Squirrel, Dove, Duck, Quail, Deer and Trap Load. There is also a Brant in the set, but it was produced for only a year or two and is very hard to find. The light tan boxes show a good likeness of the bird or animal.

In the 1940s, Remington came out with another more limited game series. These were in a dark green box and showed a duck, deer, trap, skeet and multi game pictures.

Boxes with birds or large gauge shells are sometimes shown with decoy collections where they make the display visually more interesting.

Remington Game Loads **

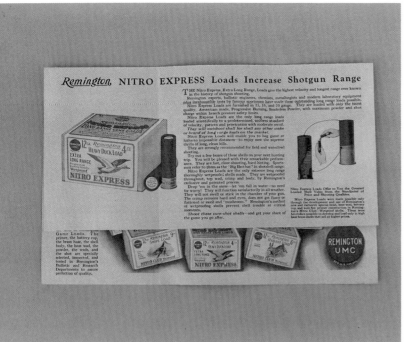

Remington Arms Company advertising folder **

Remington Arms Company ad unfolded.

Remington Squirrel Load ***

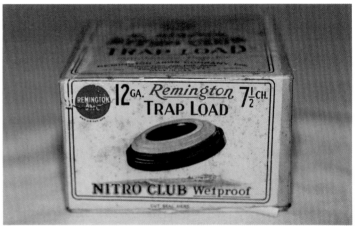

Remington Trap Load ***

Remington Quail Load ***

Remington Goose Load ***
*Ron Willoughby collection*

Remington Rabbit Load ***

Remington Heavy Duck Load ***

Remington Snipe Load ***

Remington Grouse Load ***

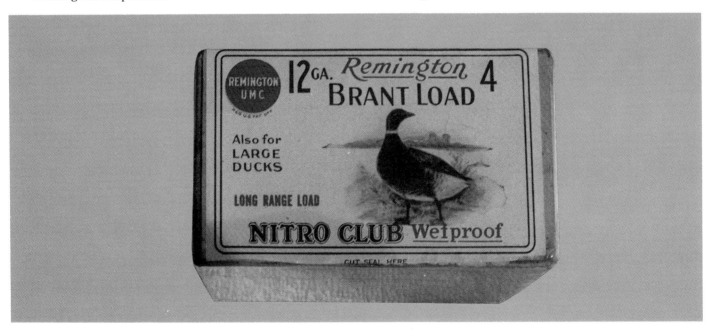

Remington Brant Load ****
*Ron Willoughby collection*

Remington UMC Buck and Duck Game Loads **

Remington UMC Kleanbore Game Loads **

Winchester NuBlack, Arrow Loaded Paper Shells
**

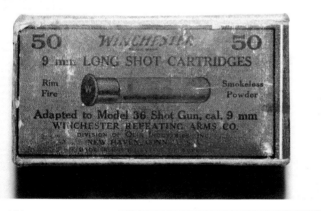 

9 mm Shot shells ***
for the Winchester Model 36 shot-
gun (garden or varmint gun) 1½
inches long

Peters High Velocity Mallard Set ***
10 gauge, 12 gauge, 16 gauge, 20
gauge, 28 gauge and 410 gauge

Boxes of 100 New Primed Empties

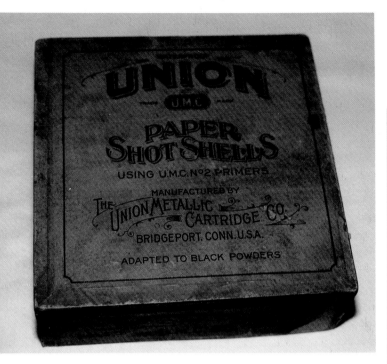

Union Metallic Cartridge Co. **
of Bridgeport, Connecticut

Robin Hood Powder Co. ***
of Swainton, Vermont

UMC Nitro Club **

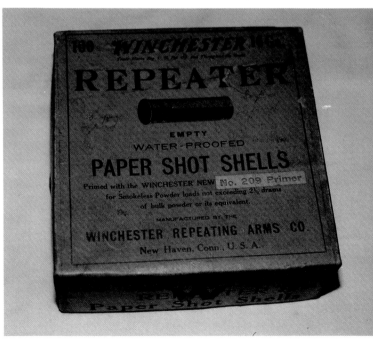

Winchester Repeating Arms Co. **
of New Haven, Connecticut

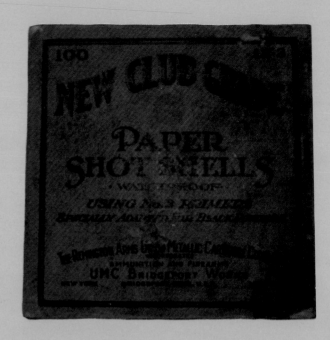

Winchester Repeating Arms Co. **

New Club Grade **

Christmas Boxes

Winchester Rival ****
*Ron Willoughby collection*

Peters Cartridge Co. ****
of Cincinnati, Ohio *Ron Willoughby collection*

Club ****
from the Union Metallic Cartridge Co. *Ron Willoughby collection*

**Club ****
from the Union Metallic Cartridge Co.**
*Ron Willoughby collection*

Red Devil ***
*Ron Willoughby collection*

Championship ***
*Ron Willoughby collection*

American Standard Loads ***
*Ron Willoughby collection*

Wm. R. Burkhard ***
*Ron Willoughby collection*

Native Son ***
*Ron Willoughby collection*

Mallard Sport load, Selby Loads **

Winchester New Rival, Defiance
Shot Shells **

Peters High
Velocity, Western
Field **

Mallard Sport Loads, Mallard Loaded Shells **

Peters Cartridge Company set of Bluebills **
Note three different addresses

Remington UMC Nitro Club set **
Note variations in labels

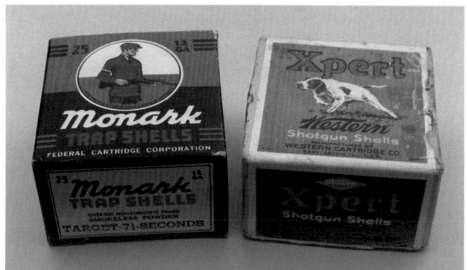

Monark, Western Xpert**

Federal Hi-Power, Nitro Express **

Opposite page
Montgomery Ward Redhead **
U.S. Cartridge Defiance

Montgomery Ward Redhead ***

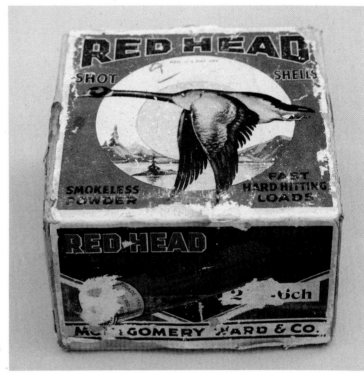

Shot shell box inserts ***

No closed season on clay birds put in flight by the DUPONT Hand Trap. You can shoot them every day in the year. Write for Hand Trap Booklet to DUPONT WILMINGTON, DEL.

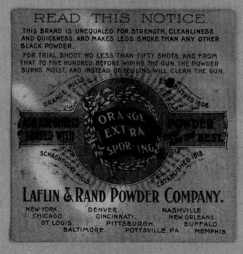

READ THIS NOTICE

THIS BRAND IS UNEQUALED FOR STRENGTH, CLEANLINESS AND QUICKNESS, AND MAKES LESS SMOKE THAN ANY OTHER BLACK POWDER.

FOR TRIAL, SHOOT NO LESS THAN FIFTY SHOTS, AND FROM THAT TO FIVE HUNDRED BEFORE WIPING THE GUN. THE POWDER BURNS MOIST, AND INSTEAD OF FOULING WILL CLEAN THE GUN.

ORANGE EXTRA SPORTING

LAFLIN & RAND POWDER COMPANY.

NEW YORK      DENVER         NASHVILLE
CHICAGO       CINCINNATI     NEW ORLEANS
ST. LOUIS     PITTSBURGH     BUFFALO
BALTIMORE     POTTSVILLE, PA.   MEMPHIS

THESE SHELLS ARE LOADED WITH
DU PONT POWDER,
MANUFACTURED BY
E.I. DU PONT de NEMOURS & CO.,
WILMINGTON, DEL.
ESTABLISHED 1802.
ORDNANCE, MILITARY AND SPORTING POWDERS
DU PONT SMOKELESS POWDER THE "RECORD BREAKER."
THE LEADING NITRO POWDER OF THE WORLD ADOPTED BY THE U.S. GOVERNMENT.

72

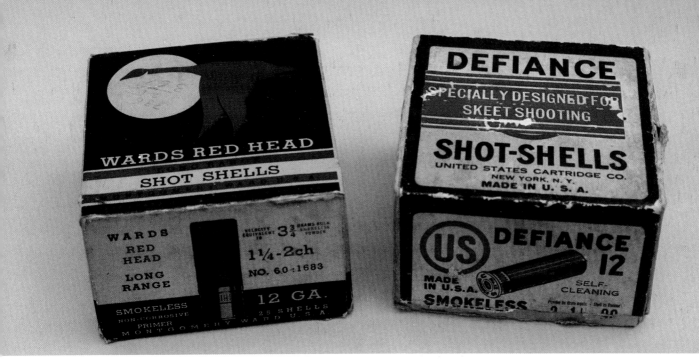

Collecting individual shells is very popular with collectors. Certain shells from particular companies and odd gauges are difficult to find. The pictures display shells from two gauge to nine millimeter. The two gauge shells were used in punt guns or yacht cannons. While I have never seen a two gauge, breach loading, punt gun, I am told that some were made in England. The English punt gun pictured here is a muzzle loader weighing 47 pounds and measuring 79 inches long. The second gun is stamped "C. C. O'Brien, Baltimore, Maryland" and is a single barrel percussion punt gun. The stamping appears on top of the barrel, on the trigger guard and on the lock plate. It has a checkered walnut stock and is 67¾ inches long. The Remington 12 gauge shown has a 14-inch extension to the magazine and holds five extra shells for use by a market hunter. The nine millimeter shells, used to shoot songbirds, fit the model 36 Winchester shot gun. The popular children's song Four and Twenty Blackbirds Baked in a Pie indicates that songbirds were hunted for food. Flickers were a popular food in Somerset County on Maryland's Eastern Shore. There Mr. J. Lloyd Sterling of Crisfield, MD carved a beautiful flicker decoy that hung on a tree.

There are many ways of organizing shot shell collections: by manufacturer, size of shell, materials (brass, paper), kind of head stamp, or oddities. There are far more paper shells than brass and they come in more sizes and, of course, colors.

Brass shells were used from the turn of the century to World War II, with the Army using brass shells on guard duty because they were not affected by the weather. The Army shells usually have a red stain over the primer and are not as desirable as the earlier shells. Brass shells were more expensive to buy, but because they could be reloaded many times they were more economical in the end. Brass shells head-stamped with the gauge and the letter "A" were to be used in guns chambered for paper shells. The letter "B" indicated they were to be used in guns chambered specifically for brass shells, and these are much more scarce. Various patents for different methods of priming and holding the wad in are also found; it is interesting to see the lengths some inventors went to get a better shell. The largest brass shell we have found is a 4 gauge, and the smallest 410, with all the usual sizes in between.

Paper shells are found in many gauges and colors by different manufacturers with various lengths of brass bases, varieties of head stamps, and experimental varieties. Books could be written covering all these possibilities. 8 gauge paper industrial shells are still used to clean kilns so beware that they were never used for hunting.

Window Shells were shells with a clear plastic window in the side. This was used by salesmen to show how the shell was loaded. They came in boxes of 5 to 7 showing different stages of manufacture. This is definitely a "find" for the avid collector.

Paper shells, 2 gauge to 8 gauge ***

UMC Co. 2½ gauge head stamp ***

UMC Co. 3 gauge head stamp ***

Remington UMC 2 gauge head stamp ***

UMC Co. 4 gauge head stamp **

UMC Co. 8 gauge head stamp **

UMC brass 4 gauge head stamp ***

Winchester brass 8 gauge head stamp **

Top Wads ***
by V.L. & D. of New York by the Steinman Hardware
Company of Lancaster, Pennsylvania and by E.K. Tryon
Jr. & Company, Philadelphia, Pennsylvania

Brass shells ***
4 gauge to 410 gauge

Tinned brass
by the Parker Company of Meridian, Connecticut 10
gauge Diamond head stamp

Remington brass 10 gauge head stamp
Note "16B" made for guns chambered for brass shells

Winchester brass 14 gauge head stamp

Head stamps
from the Robin Hood Powder Company and Knob of
Philadelphia, Pennsylvania

Assortment of paper shells
8 gauge to 9 millimeter

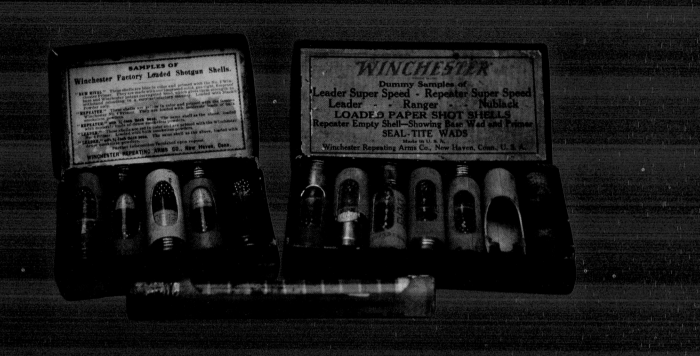

Window shells samples ***
used to show factory loading

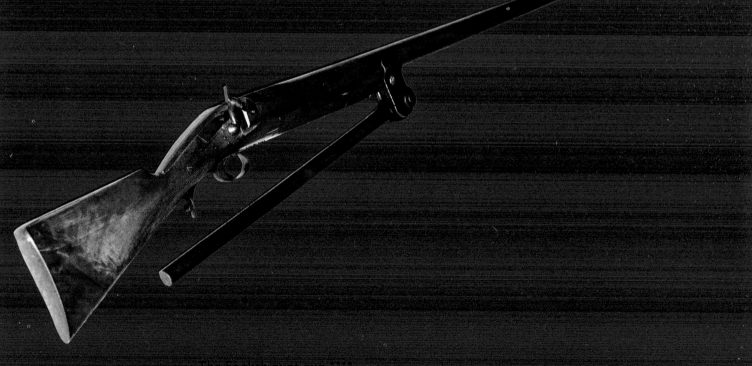

The English punt gun ***
is unmarked, is 79 inches long and weighs 47 pounds

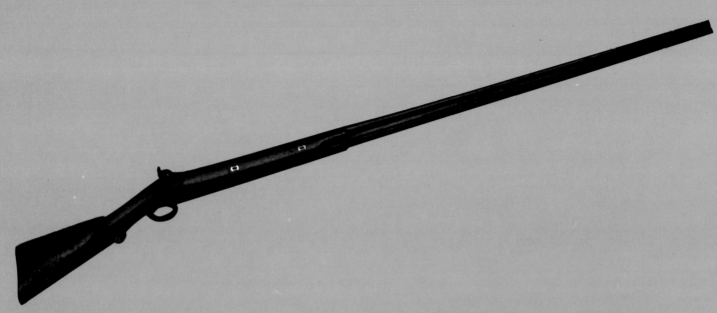

The C. C. O'Brien percussion punt gun, ****
Baltimore, Maryland, has a walnut checkered stock. The
name appears on the top of the barrel, on the trigger
guard and on the lock plate. It is 67¾ inches long.

The Remington 12-gauge with a 14-inch magazine
extension is a market hunter's gun. ***

# CHAPTER 5

# *Target Balls*

In the early 1800s, in order to improve shooting at a moving target, live pigeons were used by practicing sportsmen. The pigeons were released from traps (called ground traps) that simply opened up and released the bird, or from spring or plunge traps that threw the bird into the air. These traps are the origin of the term "trapshooting." There were many different styles of traps developed over the country. Other devices included the "gyro" trap which was a propeller-like device that whirled up from the ground, the "Belcher's Paper Bird", and the "Globe Flights", a paperboard disc open in the center with an inflated balloon that burst when hit. Today, finding these devices is all but impossible.

The first patent on glass throwers and target balls in America was issued in 1876 to Ira C. Paine. The design was derived from the sport in England. The targets were clear glass balls filled with feathers; when hit, they gave the impression of a live bird as the feathers fell.

Capt. Adam H. Bogardus, a former market hunter, became a champion target shooter. He traveled to many areas of the country demonstrating his prowess in a popular show which became well known. On November 2, 1877, in Indianapolis, Indiana, Capt. Bogardus broke 500 glass balls in 35 minutes and 4 seconds. Shortly after Paine patented his target ball, Adam Bogardus patented his own trap and target balls in April, 1877. He was a good promoter and his equipment soon became more popular than Paine's designs. The Bogardus target balls had a quilted surface and came in many colors. Now, Bogardus target ball throwers and glass balls are difficult to find. The machine was the forerunner of the clay pigeon thrower and tossed a beautiful pressed glass ball. Not many of the balls have survived; even if they were not hit, they have been broken over the years. A large variety of these balls were made by many companies, ranging in color from clear to dark blue.

Live pigeon trap ***

Adam H. Bogardus

An improvement over the glass ball was the pitch ball. Made from pitch they were much easier to see and did not leave the ground covered with glass. Another target was the Boughton smoke ball which gave off a puff of smoke when hit.

In 1880, George Ligowski invented the clay pigeon. This saucer-shaped target became popular and is still used today in many variations.

Glass target ball thrower ****
*Ron Willoughby collection*

Bogardus advertisement

Card glass target ball thrower ****

Bogardus glass target ball thrower ****
*Ron Willoughby Collection*

Clay pigeon thrower **
Chamberlin Cartridge & Target Co. *Roe Terry collection*

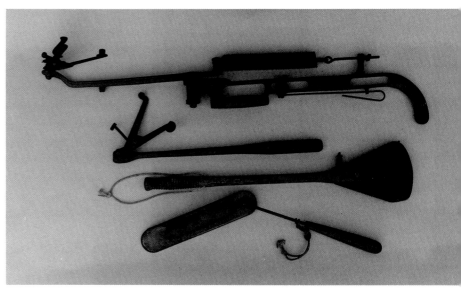

Hand Clay Pigeon Throwers **

Amber Bogardus glass target ball ***

Blue glass target ball **

Amber glass target ball **

Green glass target ball with hunter ***

Purple glass target ball with hunter ***

Purple glass target ball ***

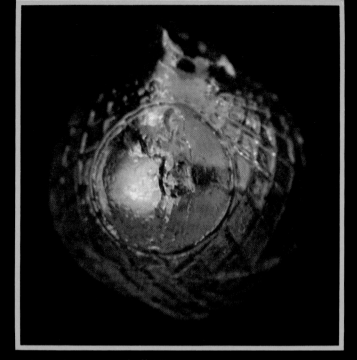

Clear glass target ball ***

Pitch target ball **

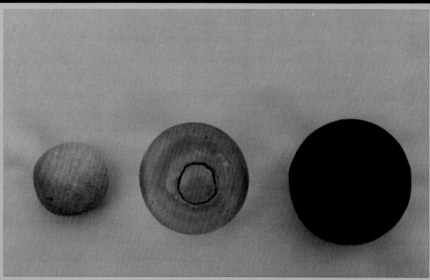

Three small target balls ***

# Licenses

Not to be overlooked in sporting collections are the licenses necessary to hunt or fish. Each state requires a license for fishing and hunting and additional stamps to hunt ducks, turkey, deer, etc. These are readily collected; there are very good references on this special subject.

BERKS COUNTY      **1914**      COUNTY No. 6

BOOK No. 5      $1.00      LICENSE No. 1172

## RESIDENT HUNTER'S LICENSE

This license is issued under the provisions of the act of April 17, 1913, entitled "An act for the better protection of wild birds and game within the Commonwealth of Pennsylvania, requiring citizens of the United States, residing within this State to procure a license before using guns for the purpose of hunting for any wild birds or animals protected by the laws of this Commonwealth, and providing penalties for violation of its several provisions," etc.

Name, Leo R. Rutter       Post Office Address, Strausstown

Height, 5ft 6in       Complexion, White

Color of Hair, Brown       Color of Eyes, Blue

Age, 17 yrs

Remarks,

This license entitles the owner thereof to hunt in any part of this Commonwealth during the game season of that calendar year in which it is issued; under the terms and prescriptions of existing law. The license is not transferable and is more in the nature of a tax receipt than a license, as it does not pretend to authorize hunting or shooting upon lands within the State contrary to the wishes of the owners thereof, or in violation of the wishes of the person controlling such lands. It does not authorize the taking or killing of animals or birds protected by any other law of the State, contrary to the provisions of that law, and permits the capture or killing of game, only during what is known as the open season for such game in this Commonwealth.

See to it that your tag number corresponds with the number of your license.

Good for the year 1914.

Issued, Oct 6 1914.

SEE TABLE OF GAME LAWS ON BACK       County Treasurer.

1914 COUNTY No. 6 LICENSE No. 1172

PENNSYLVANIA Resident Hunter's License Tag

1914 Pennsylvania hunting license ***
Cloth

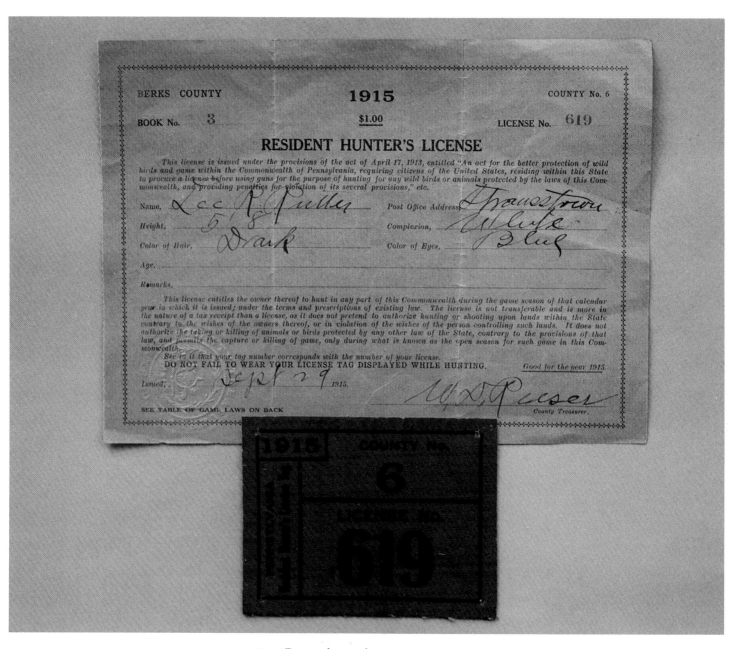

1915 Pennsylvania hunting license ***
Cloth

1924 Resident,
1931 Special, **
1937 Non Resident

1959 Antler-less Deer **
1972 Resident Senior,
1955 Fur-takers

1925-1930 Pennsylvania Hunting Licenses **

1931-1936 Pennsylvania Hunting Licenses **

Tray, Pennsylvania Fishing Licenses **

# CHAPTER 7

# *Traps*

Volcano Smokers **

Animal Trap Co.
Victor store trap display ***

Trapping for food and furs is a part of the history of mankind. In America, Indians and early settlers used traps to secure food and used the animal skins for clothing and trading. One of the earliest companies to market furs was the Hudson's Bay Company, begun with English backing for trade. And this was big business. Early trappers went west into unknown territories in search of better trapping grounds, where beaver, fox, wolf, muskrat, lynx and many other animals were in abundance. As settlers moved in, the trappers moved out. At first, traps were made with wood and animal skins. Later, styles evolved to hand-forged traps made by blacksmiths.

In 1823, Sewell I. Newhouse, a member of the religious group Oneida Community in Oneida, New York, revolutionized trapping by his perfection of the leg-hold trap. In 1882, a patent was issued to Erartus H. Hamilton, an early Oneida Community member. In 1886,

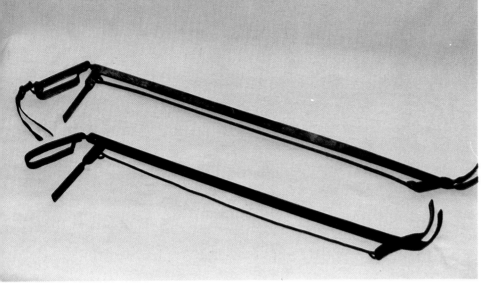

Trap setters **

Muskrat House Breaker ***
54 inches

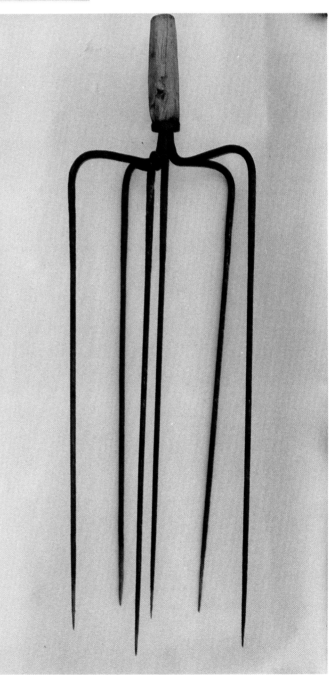

Victor Traps came on the market. 1905 marked the end of twenty-five years of making traps under the name of Oneida Community, Ltd. In 1906 Oneida purchased controlling interest in the Animal Trap Co.(ATCO) of America, and gained ownership in 1910. In 1925, Oneida Community sold its steel trap business to the Animal Trap Co. of America in Lititz, Pennsylvania. In 1939, the trap business of the Charles D. Briddel Co., Crisfield, Maryland was purchased by ATCO. In 1939, ATCO began the manufacture of duck decoys. In 1940, the Animal Trap Company of Pascagoula, Mississippi was established and started making bullet cores, fuse plugs, wrenches and wood and canvas cots for military contracts. In 1945, this part of their production ceased and they again produced traps along with decoys, containers, minnow buckets and holiday novelties adding fishing tackle, ski equipment and other items.

There are some unusual collectibles available in trapping gear. The fish and crawfish that fit over the trap pans are very nice. Trap setters and hand-forged, muskrat house breakers are other unusual items.

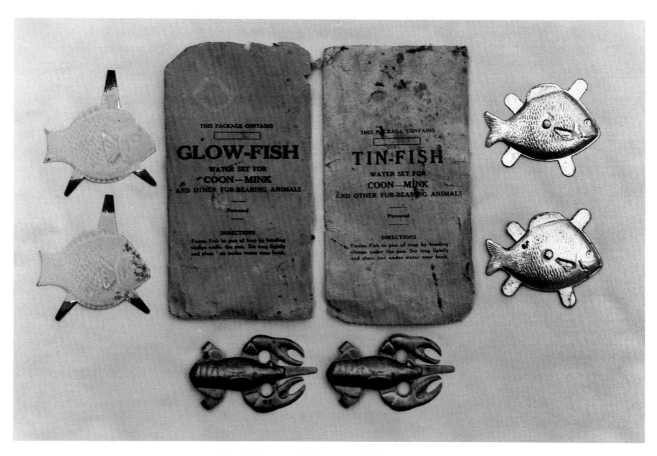

Glow fish, Tin fish, Crawfish ***
Water set for racoon and mink

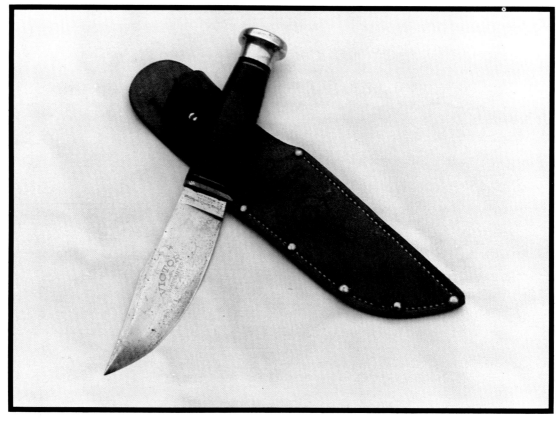

Victor skinning knife ***

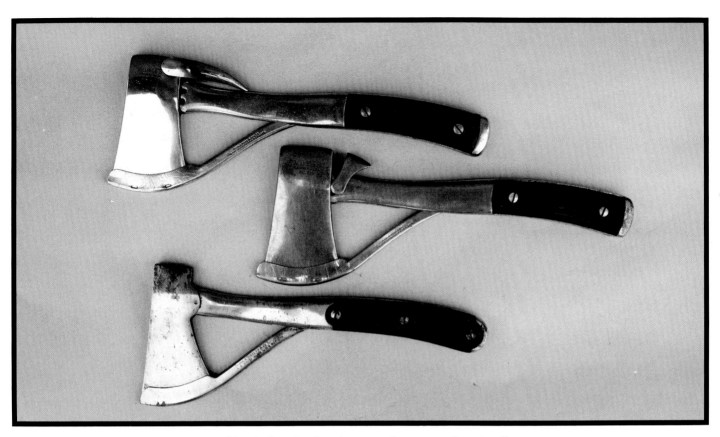

Marbles Safety Pocket Axe, number 2½ with nail puller, axe number 2P with pick, and #1 axe. *Eugene Showaker collection*

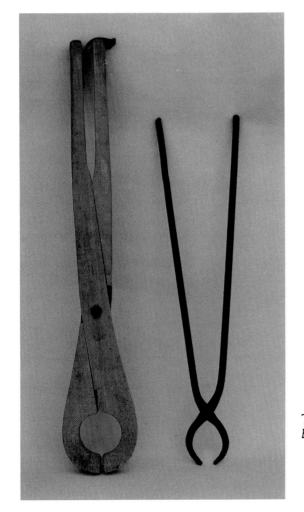

Envelopes, fur companies **

Tongs to take fox live from trap **
*Eugene Showaker collection*

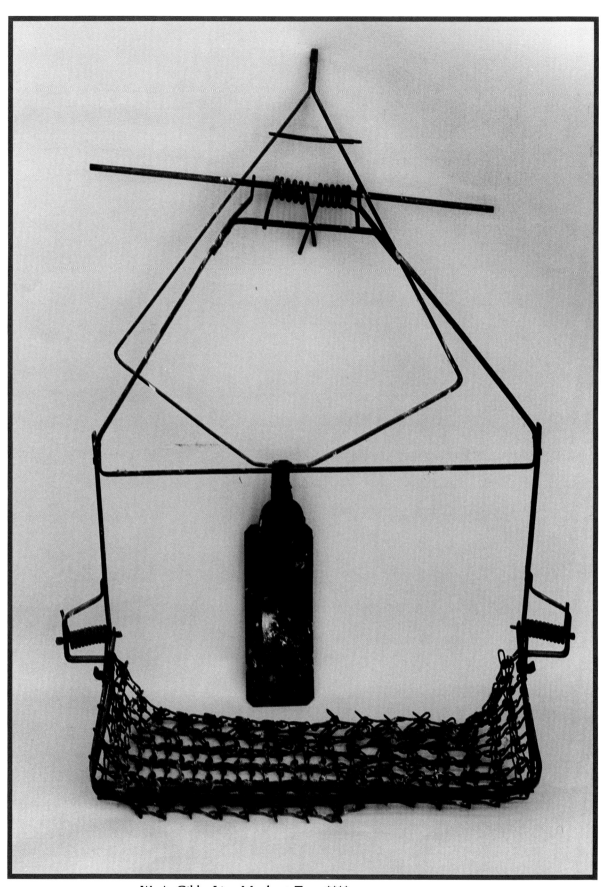

W. A. Gibbs Live Muskrat Trap ★★★★
Used to trap live muskrats for breeding purposes *Eugene
Showaker collection*

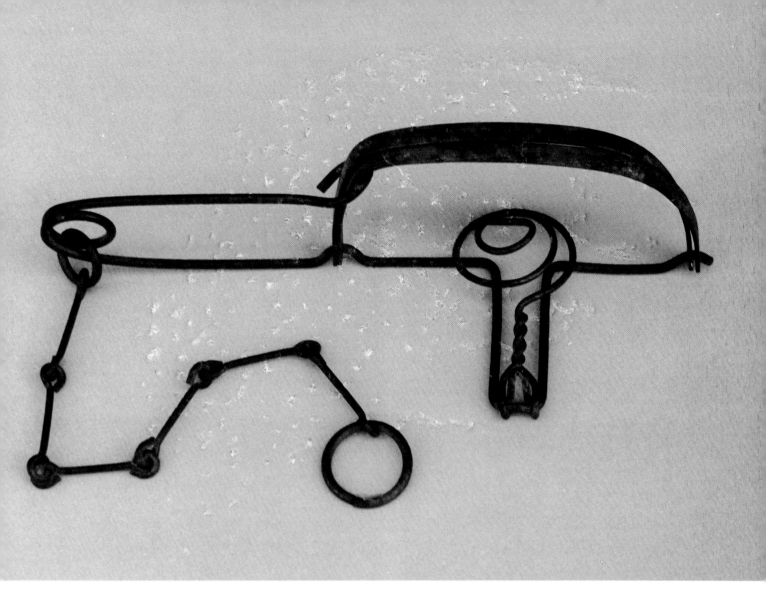

Unusual rat trap ****
*Eugene Showaker collection*

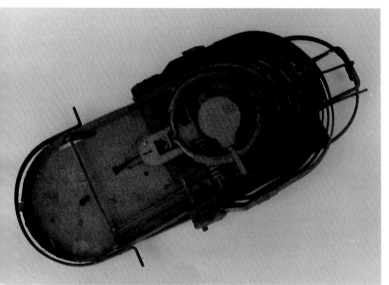

W.A. Gibbs Live Muskrat Trap **
Trap shown as it is set *Eugene Showaker collection*

W. A. Gibbs Live Muskrat Trap
Trap shown as when sprung *Eugene Showaker collection*

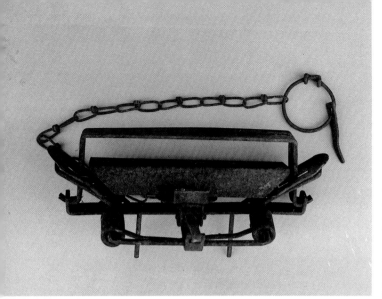

**W. A. Gibbs Hawk and Owl Trap** **
*Eugene Showaker collection*

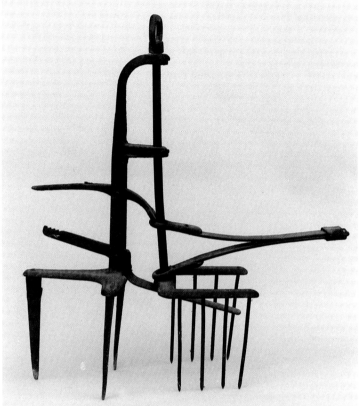

**Mole Trap** ***
*Eugene Showaker collection*

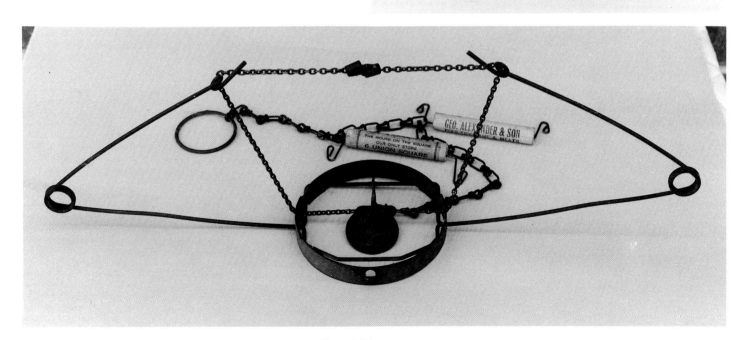

**Wasson Humane Trap** ****
Emerson Apparatus Co. *Eugene Showaker collection*

First Hunter Trapper Trader Magazine, October 1900 ****, March 1932 ** *Eugene Showaker collection*

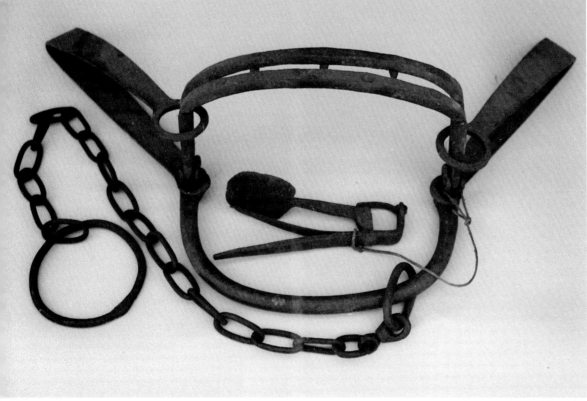

D. M. Woodcock Bear Trap *** Special half circle base also used to carry over the shoulder. *Eugene Showaker collection*

Mass & Steffen Fur Co. 1937 Calendar **
"Friendly Greetings" by Jack Murray *Eugene Showaker collection*

Mass & Steffen Fur Co. 1941 Calendar **
"The Engineer" by Jack Murray *Eugene Showaker collection*

Funsten Bros & Co. watch fob ***
*Eugene Showaker collection*

Hunter Trapper Trader watch fob **
Hunter Trapper Trader watch fob with compass ****
*Eugene Showaker collection*

Back of Funsten watch fob

National Sportsman fobs **
*Eugene Showaker collection*

Sears Raw Furs, Abrahams Furs, **
S. Silberman Furs and Northwestern Fur *Eugene Showaker collection*

Dead Shot watch fobs **
*Eugene Showaker collection*

Skinning knife sharpeners **
Clay Export Co., Chicago
W. R. Adams, Fremont, NE
*Eugene Showaker collection*

Knife sharpeners **
*Eugene Showaker collection*

# CHAPTER 8

# *Sporting Books*

Sporting collectors hunt in book shows, auction sales, yard sales and at rare book dealers for works by particular authors or illustrators. We started by collecting books illustrated by Lynn Bogue Hunt who wrote and illustrated wildlife books, the most famous being **An Artist's Game Bag** published by Derrydale Press, one of the most famous publishers of sporting books. Hunt was also a duck stamp design winner in 1939-40, which made him very popular.

Archibald Rutledge,(a professor at Mercersburg Academy in Pennsylvania, and resident at his plantation, Hampton, in South Carolina,) wrote of his experiences in the field, both in South Carolina and Pennsylvania. His stories about the outdoors should be included on all sportsmen's lists.

Ray Holland, the editor of **Field and Stream** magazine wrote two wonderful books, **Shooting in the Uplands** and **Shooting in the Lowlands.** These are also illustrated by Lynn Bogue Hunt.

**A Sportsman of the Old South** is a most enjoyable book. Written by Harry Worcester Smith, it speaks of his ancestors, especially Frederick Gustavus Skinner, who knew about hunting prior to the Civil War. Skinner was a Colonel in the First Virginia Regiment, Confederate States of America, and writer and Editor for **Turf, Field and Farm Magazine**. He also started the first register of horses in America. Skinner projects an interesting ante-bellum point of view in his stories about aristocrats hunting and his opinion that only the wealthy should be allowed to hunt because only they could afford a good dog and a good gun.

Another writer, Zane Grey, popularized many books on fishing as well as Western stories. He used the income from his western novels to finance his worldwide fishing trips, and then wrote about his adventures.

A good book on the early powder companies is **DuPont, One Hundred and Forty Years** by William S.Dutton, (Scribners, 1942). This lists many old powder companies purchased by the DuPont Co.

A good library can keep a collector occupied during the times he cannot be out looking for new acquisitions.

Assortment of sporting books **

# CHAPTER 9

# *Paper Arts*

**Posters. Postcards. Envelopes. Letterheads. Magazines and Newspapers.**

Game's Worst Enemy **
Pennsylvania Game Commission *P. Majerich, Jr. collection*

Help Wildlife **
Pennsylvania Game Commission *P. Majerich, Jr. collection*

Posters from your state's Department of Forest and Waters, Game Commission and Fish Commission are interesting to collect. During the Depression of the 1930s, the arts were kept alive by the government-sponsored Work Projects Administration (W.P.A.) which commissioned artists to do work for political entities. The W.P.A. paid artists to create posters for state conservation agencies. This was quality work and these posters, by artists like Joe Wolf and Jacob Bates Abbott, are purchased by art collectors today.

Postcards, envelopes and letterheads from the many powder companies, shot shell manufacturers, and regional dealers are part of the histories of these companies. Also, postcards with the old sink box hunters and many from areas where hunting took place can be found.

Magazines and newspapers are collected for cover pictures, stories by well-known authors, and information contained in the advertisements. Many times, authors compiled a number of their stories into books. For example, the first article on decoys was written by Joel Barber ( **A History of Duck Decoys**),in the December, 1928 issue of **Field and Stream**. This and another article (**Add Americana: The Decoy**) in the August 1932 issue of **Fortune Magazine** later became parts of his **Wildfowl Decoys**, published in 1934, which was the first book on collecting decoys.

The Open Gate To Mutual Understanding **
Pennsylvania Game Commission *P. Majerich, Jr. collection*

Help Feed and Care for our Game **
Pennsylvania Game Commission *P. Majerich, Jr. collection*

Hunters Be Considerate to Host—The Farmer **
Pennsylvania Game Commission *P. Majerich, Jr. collection*

Rabbit Farm**
Pennsylvania Game Commission *P. Majerich, Jr. collection*

Don't Be a Game Hog **
Pennsylvania Game Commission *P. Majerich, Jr. collection*

Stealing Traps is Dastardly **
Pennsylvania Game Commission *P. Majerich, Jr. collection*

Hunters Help Feed Your Game **
Pennsylvania Game Commission *P. Majerich, Jr. collection*

Forest Fires Destroy Game **
Game Commissioners of Pennsylvania *P. Majerich, Jr. collection*

Game News **
Pennsylvania Game News *P. Majerich, Jr. collection*

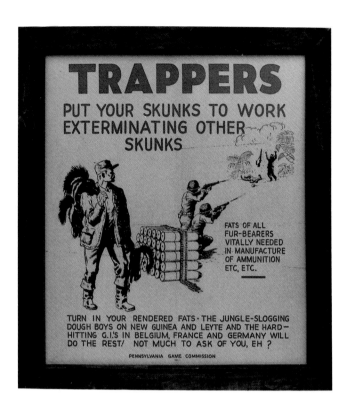

Trappers Put Your Skunks to Work **
Pennsylvania Game Commission *P. Majerich, Jr. collection*

Protect Our Birds **
Pennsylvania Game News *P. Majerich, Jr. collection*

Logo, Jacob Bates Abbott *P. Majerich, Jr. collection*

Logo, Joe Wolf *P. Majerich, Jr. collection*

After Spraying **
Pennsylvania Fish Commission *P. Majerich, Jr. collection*

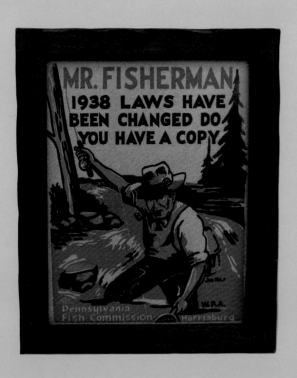

Mr. Fisherman **
Joe Wolf WPA *P. Majerich, Jr. collection*

Help Protect Forests From Fire **
Department of Forest and Waters
Note human pose of tree *P. Majerich, Jr. collection*

Pennsylvania Fish Commission Seal ***
*P. Majerich, Jr. collection*

Commonwealth of Pennsylvania Citation ***
to Henry C. Ford *P. Majerich, Jr. collection*

Pennsylvania Fish Commission metal sign ***

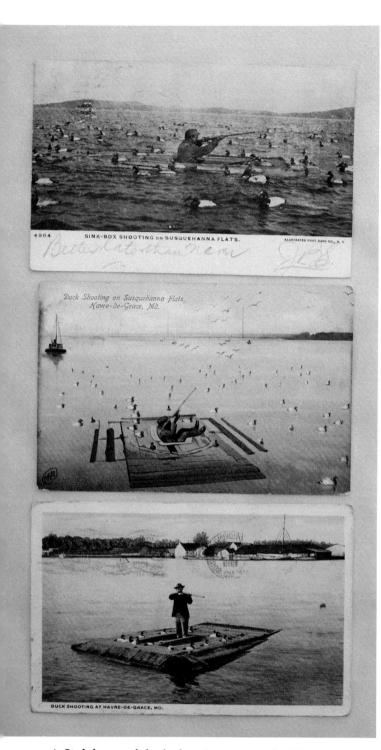

A Sink box and duck shooting postcards ***

Stereopticon pictures of hunting scenes **
Note field decoys on top picture

Stereopticon pictures of hunting scenes **

106

Stereopticon scenes of hunters and game **

Envelopes, Winchester repeating shotguns **
Hunter Arms Co.

Envelopes, U.S. Ammunition, **
Remington guns and rifles

*Harpers Weekly* hunting scene **
"Rail Shooting on the Delaware"

American Powder Mills letterhead **

Early magazines: *The American Angler* **
*Shooting and Fishing*

*A History of Duck Decoys*

December, 1928 issue of *Field and Stream* **
with author Joel Barber's first article on decoys

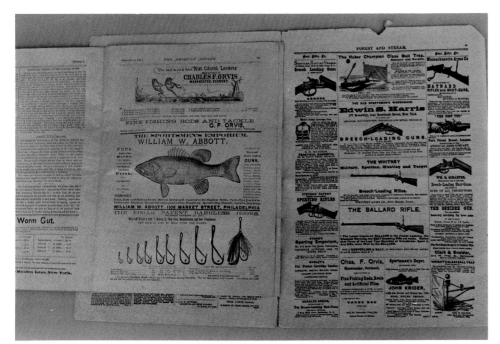

Advertisements from early magazines **

Magazines: *National Sportsman* **
*Field and Stream*

Magazines: *All Outdoors* **
*Outdoor Life*

109

Early magazines: *American Field* **
*Forest and Stream*

August, 1932 issue of *Fortune Magazine* **
with author Joel Barber's second article on decoys

Add Americana: *The Decoy*

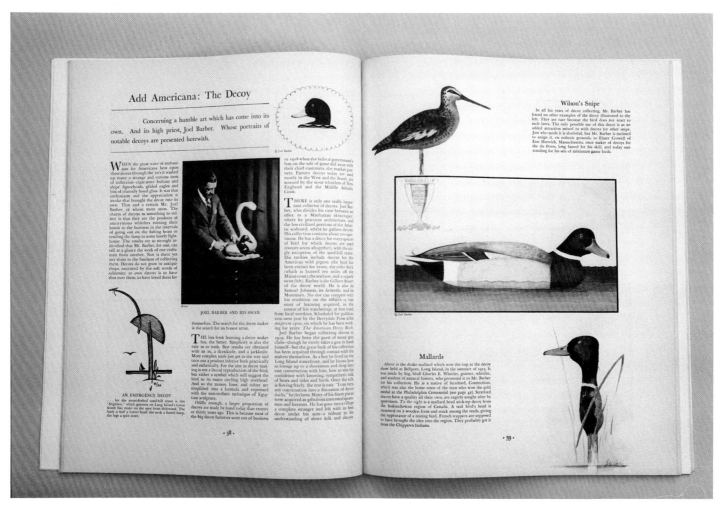

# CHAPTER 10

# *Sporting Prints*

Sporting prints have been produced for many years. A. B. Frost, considered a sportsman's artist, was one of the earliest and most popular. His **Shooting Pictures** portfolio, published in 1895 by Charles Scribner's Sons, is a set of twelve lithographs of various hunting scenes including: "Autumn Grouse,""Autumn Woodcock," "Quail a Dead Stand," "Quail a Covey Rise," "Rabbit Shooting," "Summer Woodcock," "Duck Shooting From a Blind," "Duck Shooting From a Battery," "Rail Shooting," "Prairie Shooting," "English Snipe," and "Bay Snipe." In 1903, Scribner published another of his portfolios called **A Day's Shooting** which had six prints: "Good Luck," "Bad Luck," "Ordered Off," "Gun Shy," "Smoking Them Out," and "We've Got Him." Frost always added a bit of humor in his pictures.

As mentioned earlier, Lynn Bogue Hunt was a painter of wildlife who is famous for his game birds and game fish. In 1917, you could purchase a set of eighteen **Our American Game Birds** prints from the DuPont Company illustrated by Lynn Bogue Hunt. On the back of each is a description of the birds and a chart giving the size shot and amount of powder to be used for each game. In 1944, **Field and Stream** published a folio of twelve **Game Birds of America** prints and also a folio of six **Fishing in America** prints. What a prize when you find a set with the descriptive folder included!

Edwin Megargee was a famous artist known for his dog paintings. The **Field and Stream** Portfolio called **Gun Dogs At Work** included: "The Cocker Spaniel,""The Springer Spaniel," "The English Setter," "The Chesapeake Bay Retriever," "The Pointer," and "The Labrador Retriever."

Among other wildlife artists, favorites include Richard E. Bishop, Roland H. Clark, Francis Lee Jaques, Maynard Reece and Louis Frisino.

A. B. Frost's shooting pictures **
18½ by 12½ inches overall

A. B. Frost *Shooting Ducks From A Blind* **

*Shooting Ducks from a Blind*

*Shooting Ducks from a Battery*

A. B. Frost
*Shooting Ducks From A Battery* **

A. B. Frost *Bay Snipe* **

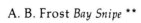

*Bay Snipe*

Complete set of 1944 *Field and Stream* **
*Game Birds of America*
Lynn Bogue Hunt prints
12⅜ by 16 1/16 inches overall

*Diving Ducks* **
*Canada Geese*
*Brant and Pintail*

*Ring Neck Pheasant* **
*Mourning Dove and Bob White*

*Tarpon, Large-mouth Bass* \*\*

*Field and Stream,* 1944 \*\*
*Fishing in America*
Lynn Bogue Hunt prints

*Bob White* \*\*
*Upland Plover, Hudsonian Curlew*

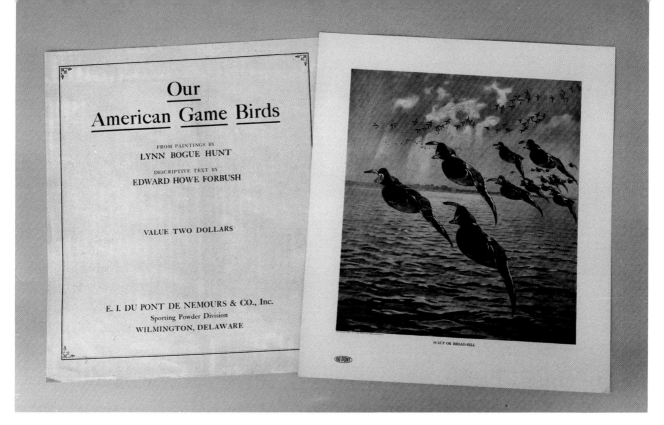

Complete set, 1917, duPont ***

*Our American Game Birds*
Lynn Bogue Hunt prints
*Scaup or Broadbill*
13 by 14½ inches overall

Small enclosure book ***
included with *Our American Game Birds*, 6¼ by 7½
inches

Currier & Ives lithographs: ***
*Beach Snipe Hunting*
28½ by 22¾ inches overall

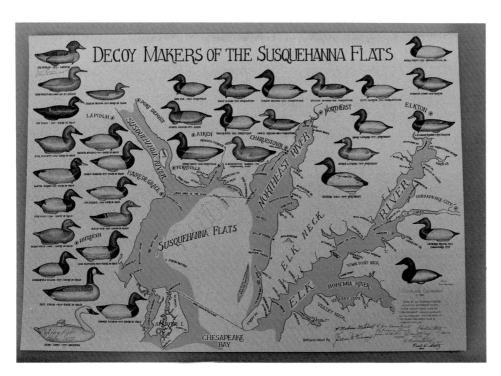

*Decoy Makers of the Susquehanna Flats* **
Paul Shertz, 34 by 24 inches

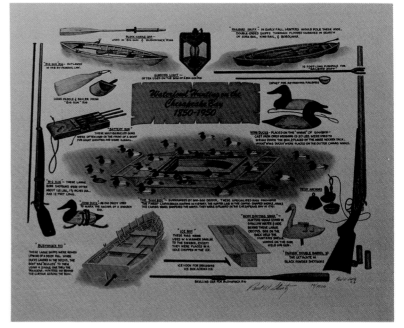

*Waterfowl Hunting on the Chesapeake Bay* **
Paul Shertz, 23 by 19 inches

# CHAPTER 11

# *Advertisements*

Collecting sporting advertisements is very exciting. These items of paper, wood and tin usually can be dated.

The paper items include calendars, postcards, trade cards, letterheads, billheads, and point-of-display advertising. The wooden items include shot shell, oyster and fish boxes. Tin items include pin backs (lapel pins), signs, fish tins, and oyster and crabmeat cans. The pinbacks have pictures of many shooting personalities and the logos of gun and powder companies.

Animal Trap Co., ***
Victor duck head paper weight

Winchester paper weight ***

Animal Trap Co. **
Victor decoy advertising

Assorted pin backs **

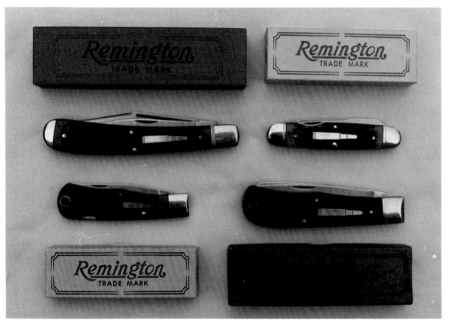

Reissue Remington bullet knives *

Seafood Cans **

Seafood packing house employee tokens **

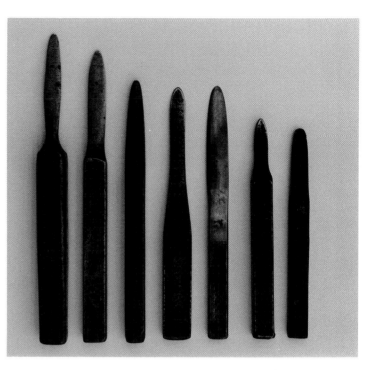

Oyster shucking knives **

Wooden Mason decoy shipping box ****
19½ inches high, 30¼ inches long, 22 inches wide

Wooden shot shell boxes *

Wooden shot shell boxes *

8-gauge shot shell box ***

Oyster packing wooden boxes **

Southern Sea Food Co. shipping box **

Surf City Fishery shipping box *

1914 Robin Hood Coin ***

Reverse side of the coin with the 1914 Game Laws for the state of Pennsylvania

Animal Trap Co. **
Victor decoys and accessories advertisement

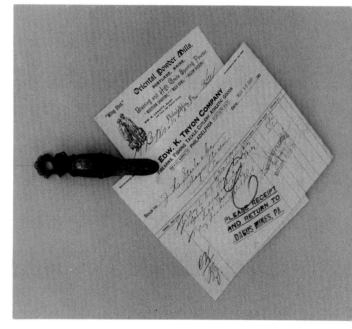

Duck paper clip with sporting billheads **

John Krider broadside ***

Gun catalogs **

Cover of the DuPont Game Register ***

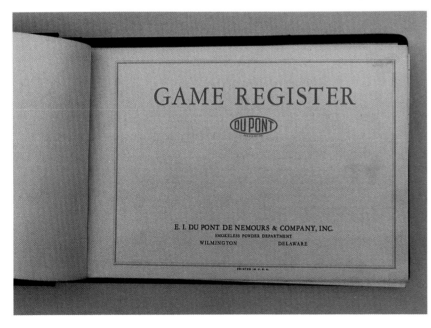

Shooting register

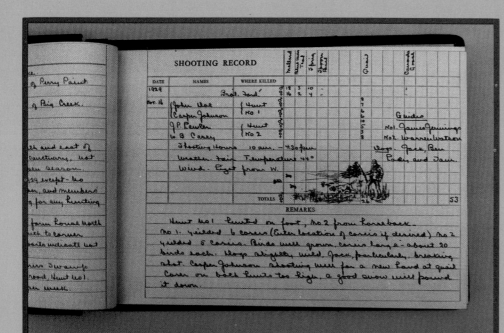

Shooting record

U. S. shot shells **
*They're packed with power, 16 by 28 inches*

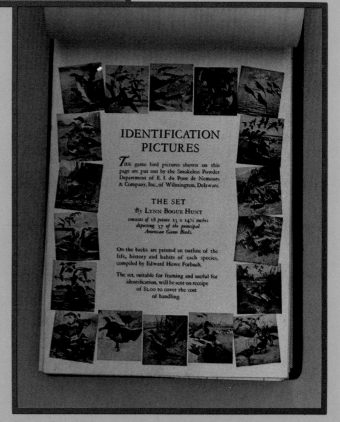

Lynn Bogue Hunt pictures in DuPont Game Register

U. S. Defiance—Ajax Heavies **
18 by 19½ inches

U.S. Ammunition ***
*Come on, what ails yer!*, 58 by 41 inches

U.S. shot shells ****
*A load for every purpose, a shell for every purse*
note boat separate across middle 62 by 34½ inches

U. S. Ammunition ***
*Raven Mad,*
58½ by 40 inches

Kleanbore shot shells **
10½ by 6 inches

Kleanbore shot shells **
12½ by 21½ inches

Remington UMC ***
*For Shooting Right*
52 by 31 inches

Remington UMC ***
*Old Boy! We have the winning combination for tomorrow* 50½ by
35 inches

# CHAPTER 12

# *Hanging Game Pictures*

The hanging trophies of a hunt became a popular Victorian subject. A carry-over from the European custom of hanging live game on a barn or board, the pictures were first made by painting and carving wooden game, and later, in order to make them available to the average household, some were cast in metal and many were made from impressed cardboard to give the illusion of three dimensions. One series even has a fly embossed along with the game. These were highly colored and served as decoration in many Victorian homes.

Ducks and fish **

Pair of cast metal duck plaques ***

Songbirds **

Shorebirds **

Pheasants **

# CHAPTER 13

# Glassware and China

Pressed glass made in the United States after the Civil War included patterns relating to the history of the country. Birds and animals depicted in pressed glass are very rare. The Bird and Strawberry pattern originally was made in many pieces from punch cups to bowls, wines and compotes.

Among the pressed glass patterns with sporting subjects are **Ostrich Looking at the Moon** which shows an ostrich wearing a pince-nez looking at the moon. Other such patterns include:

**Frog & Spider**      **Lion**
**Owl and Possum**     **Dragon**
**Deer and Dog**       **Deer and Pine Tree**
**Cardinal**           **Birds in the Swamp**
**Pigs in the Corn**   **Flying Stork**

These are a sample of the wonderful patterns glass companies created to provide something different.

A collector might decide to collect one pattern or one piece in all the different patterns. Some people serve guests with the different tumblers or wine glasses which makes a very interesting table setting. The patterns **Horse, Cat and Rabbit** and **Jumbo** are beautiful with the clearest mold markings. **Beaver Band**, which is very desired, was made in Canada.

Covered dishes in animal patterns are also popular items which were used as containers for mustard or other condiments. They came in a variety of animal subjects and the detail is very beautiful.

Lobster milk pitcher, ***
and cream pitcher by Royal Bayreuth *Richard Chubb collection*

Lobster celery dish and individual salts ***
by Royal Bayreuth *Richard Chubb collection*

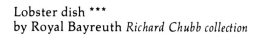

Lobster dish ***
by Royal Bayreuth *Richard Chubb collection*

The Imperial Glass Company of Bellaire, Ohio manufactured a set of depression glasses made to look like shot shells. They were made in both green and red and were trimmed in gold or silver. The tall, tankard-style pitcher had a wooden stirrer that looked like a gun-cleaning rod and was called a "magnum". The iced tea glass was called "big shot", the tumbler was called "sure shot", the juice was called "half shot" and the shot glass was called "little shot". Placed with a collection of decoys, these add color and can be put to use while viewing a collection!

The Heisey Glass Co. of Newark, Ohio, and the Cambridge Glass Co. of Cambridge, Ohio manufactured some unusual pieces with bird and animal motifs.

Ceramics companies also produced beautiful pieces decorated with birds and animals. Seagrams, Inc. had a set of plates available to the public. Sporting clubs had plates made for special presentations.

In the late 1940's, The Alfred Meakins Company manufactured a set of plates decorated with prints of Audubon Birds, and Johnson Brothers had a Game Bird and Fish series. Noritake made some lovely Game Bird china, all very collectible.

The Royal Bayreuth factory was established in Tettau, Bavaria in 1794. Animal and other unusual figural shapes were made there between 1885 and the beginning of World War I (1914). The many colorful figural pieces make Royal Bayreuth ceramics highly collectible today.

Elk milk pitcher, **
and cream pitcher by Royal Bayreuth *Richard Chubb collection*

Shell cream pitcher, lobster cream pitcher, and lettuce cream pitcher with lobster handle**
by Royal Bayreuth *Richard Chubb collection*

Lobster mustard pot and two compotes ***
by Royal Bayreuth *Richard Chubb collection*

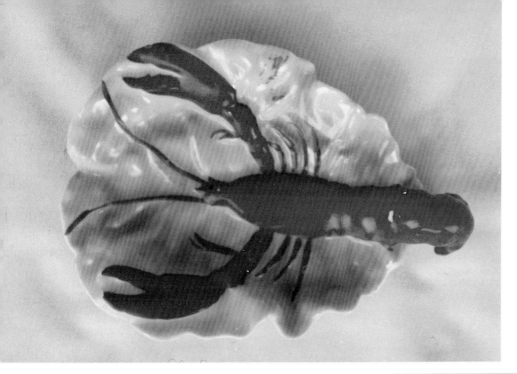

Lettuce and lobster candy dish ***
by Royal Bayreuth *Richard Chubb collection*

Royal Bayreuth company logo

Eagle cream pitcher, ***
and owl cream pitcher by Royal Bayreuth Richard
Chubb

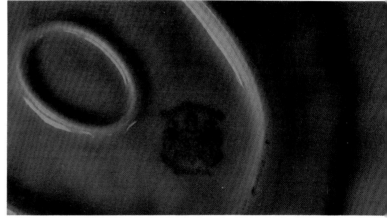

Frog cream pitcher, ****
and alligator cream pitcher by Royal
Bayreuth *Richard Chubb collection*

Elk toothpick holder ***
by Royal Bayreuth *Richard Chubb collection*

Lynn Bogue Hunt designed plates ***
made for the Quaker City Gun Club,
Philadelphia, PA

Shorebird plate **
by Seagram, Inc.

Fish plate **
by Seagram, Inc.

Octopus oyster plate **

Songbird oyster plate **

135

George Jones Majolica covered
fish dish ****
with silver Tiffany & Co. insert,
24 inches long

Shot shell pitcher and glasses, red **
by Imperial Glass Co., Bellaire, Ohio

Shot shell pitcher and glasses, green **
by Imperial Glass Co., Bellaire, Ohio

Jumbo and Barnum covered sugar bowl ***
Showman P. T. Barnum's head is at the bottom of the
handle.

Fish design tankard pitcher ****
by Cambridge Glass Co., Cambridge, Ohio

Fish design water glass ****
by Cambridge Glass Co., Cambridge, Ohio

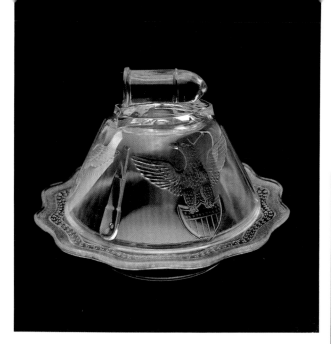

Bullet and patriotic emblem covered butter ***
Made in 1898, this pattern commemorates the
Spanish-American War

Peacock pattern tankard pitcher ****
Cambridge Glass Co.

Green Aquarium pattern pitcher ***

Swan pattern covered sugar ***
Clear non-flint glass made in the 1880s.

Celery dish with butterfly handles ***
made in the 1880s

Crystal heron flower holder **
made by Cambridge Glass Co.

Lion and Baboon pattern cream pitcher ***
a humorous design of the 1880s

Bird and Strawberry pattern goblet ****
made in the 1890s

Frosted Polar Bear pattern goblet **
made in the 1870s

Late Butterfly design wine glass ***
made in the late 1890s to look like cut glass

Milk glass Fox pattern covered dish ***
with a duck in the fox's mouth

Milk glass Attebury Duck
Patented March 15, 1887

Milk glass Crawfish pattern covered dish **

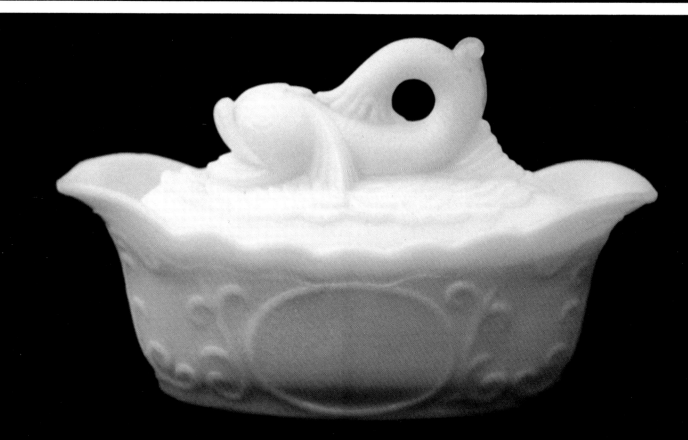

Milk glass Dolphin pattern covered dish **

# CHAPTER 14

# *Stamps*

When the Migratory Bird Hunting Stamp Act was passed in July, 1934, Mr. Jay N. Darling (nicknamed "Ding") designed the first stamp titled "Mallards Dropping In". He was president of the National Wildlife Federation and in 1934 was Chief of the U. S. Bureau of Biological Survey. Nearly all the money derived from the sale of the duck stamps has been used to purchase and maintain waterfowl refuges. For years, the Bureau extended invitations to wildlife artists to design each year's new stamp. In 1949-50, the Bureau announced that any artist could compete for the stamp design with the winner receiving a plate of stamps in a presentation folder, prestige, and the right to publish prints from the original painting. All the issued stamps depict wildfowl except the 1959-60 stamp which shows a Labrador retriever, and the 1975-76 stamp which shows a duck decoy. Recent rule changes now require the subject be a living waterfowl. An excellent way of displaying collected stamps is in the **Catalog of the Duck Stamp Prints with Biographies of the Artists** compiled by Jean Pride Stearns and revised by Russell A. Fink. Here each page is designed for a particular stamp with a brief biography and picture of the artist. This album protects the stamps yet they can be seen easily.

Other stamps and prints have been issued by state agencies, particularly for wildfowl, but also for trout, turkey and other game. Private organizations also printed stamps and posters as fund raisers and they are often found in sporting collections.

*A Catalog of the Duck Stamp Prints* *
*with biographies of the artists* by Jean Pride Stearns revised by Russell A. Fink

*Mallards Dropping In* ***
by Jay "Ding" Darling, 1934-35

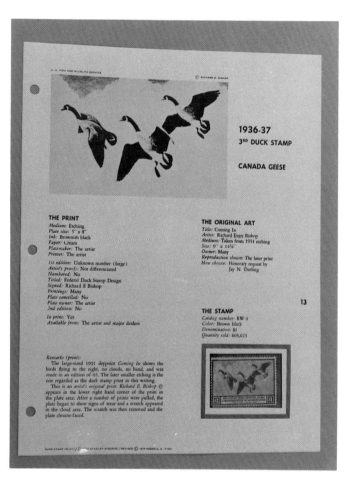

*Coming In* **
by Robert Everett Bishop, 1936-37

*Pintails* **
by Roland Hanmer Clark, 1938-39

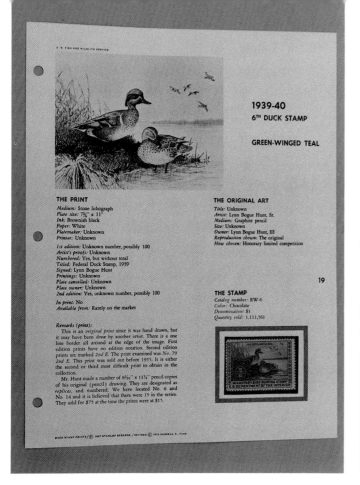

**1939-40**

**6TH DUCK STAMP**

**GREEN-WINGED TEAL**

**THE PRINT**
*Medium:* Stone lithograph
*Plate size:* 7¾" x 11"
*Ink:* Brownish black
*Paper:* White
*Platemaker:* Unknown
*Printer:* Unknown

*1st edition:* Unknown number, possibly 100
*Artist's proofs:* Unknown
*Numbered:* Yes, but without total
*Titled:* Federal Duck Stamp, 1939
*Signed:* Lynn Bogue Hunt
*Printings:* Unknown
*Plate cancelled:* Unknown
*Plate owner:* Unknown
*2nd edition:* Yes, unknown number, possibly 100

*In print:* No
*Available from:* Rarely on the market

**Remarks (print):**
    This is an *original* print since it was hand drawn, but it may have been done by another artist. There is a one line border all around at the edge of the image. First edition prints have an edition notation. Second edition prints are marked *2nd E.* The print examined was *No. 79 2nd E.* This print was sold out before 1955. It is either the second or third most difficult print to obtain in the collection.
    Mr. Hunt made a number of 8½" x 11½" pencil copies of his original (pencil) drawing. They are designated as *replicas,* and numbered. We have located No. 6 and No. 14 and it is believed that there were 15 in the series. They sold for $75 at the time the prints were at $15.

**THE ORIGINAL ART**
*Title:* Unknown
*Artist:* Lynn Bogue Hunt, Sr.
*Medium:* Graphite pencil
*Size:* Unknown
*Owner:* Lynn Bogue Hunt, III
*Reproduction shown:* The original
*How chosen:* Honorary limited competition

19

**THE STAMP**
*Catalog number:* RW-6
*Color:* Chocolate
*Denomination:* $1
*Quantity sold:* 1,111,561

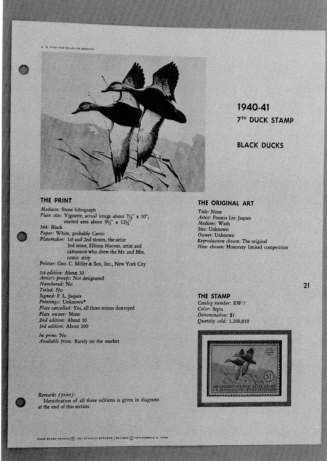

**1940-41**

**7TH DUCK STAMP**

**BLACK DUCKS**

**THE PRINT**
*Medium:* Stone lithograph
*Plate size:* Vignette, actual image about 7¼" x 10", matted area about 9½" x 12½"
*Ink:* Black
*Paper:* White, probably *Curtis*
*Platemaker:* 1st and 2nd stones, the artist
        3rd stone, Ellison Hoover, artist and
        cartoonist who drew the Mr. and Mrs.
        comic strip
*Printer:* Geo. C. Miller & Son, Inc., New York City

*1st edition:* About 30
*Artist's proofs:* Not designated
*Numbered:* No
*Titled:* No
*Signed:* F. L. Jaques
*Printings:* Unknown*
*Plate cancelled:* Yes, all three stones destroyed
*Plate owner:* None
*2nd edition:* About 30
*3rd edition:* About 200

*In print:* No
*Available from:* Rarely on the market

**THE ORIGINAL ART**
*Title:* None
*Artist:* Francis Lee Jaques
*Medium:* Wash
*Size:* Unknown
*Owner:* Unknown
*Reproduction shown:* The original
*How chosen:* Honorary limited competition

21

**THE STAMP**
*Catalog number:* RW-7
*Color:* Sepia
*Denomination:* $1
*Quantity sold:* 1,260,810

**Remarks (print):**
    Identification of all three editions is given in diagrams at the end of this section.

*Green-Winged Teal* **
by Lynn Bogue Hunt, 1939-40

*King Buck* (a dog) **
by Maynard Reece, 1959-60

*Black Ducks* **
by Francis Lee Jaques, 1940-41

*Buffleheads Aloft* **
by Maynard Reece, 1948-49

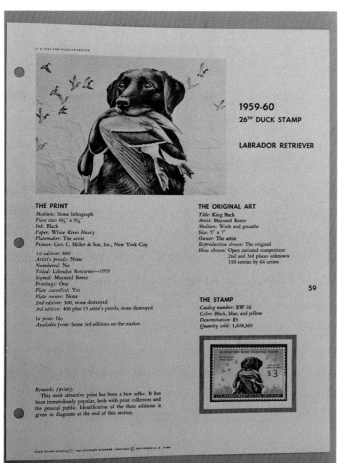

**1959-60**

**26TH DUCK STAMP**

**LABRADOR RETRIEVER**

**THE PRINT**
*Medium:* Stone lithograph
*Plate size:* 6½" x 9½"
*Ink:* Black
*Paper:* White Rives Heavy
*Platemaker:* The artist
*Printer:* Geo. C. Miller & Son, Inc., New York City

*1st edition:* 400
*Artist's proofs:* None
*Numbered:* No
*Titled:* Labrador Retriever—1959
*Signed:* Maynard Reece
*Printings:* One
*Plate cancelled:* Yes
*Plate owner:* None
*2nd edition:* 300, stone destroyed
*3rd edition:* 400 plus 15 artist's proofs, stone destroyed

*In print:* No
*Available from:* Some 3rd editions on the market.

**THE ORIGINAL ART**
*Title:* King Buck
*Artist:* Maynard Reece
*Medium:* Wash and gouache
*Size:* 5" x 7"
*Owner:* The artist
*Reproduction shown:* The original
*How chosen:* Open national competition
        2nd and 3rd places unknown
        110 entries by 64 artists

59

**THE STAMP**
*Catalog number:* RW-26
*Color:* Black, blue, and yellow
*Denomination:* $3
*Quantity sold:* 1,628,365

**Remarks (print):**
    This most attractive print has been a best seller. It has been tremendously popular, both with print collectors and the general public. Identification of the three editions is given in diagrams at the end of this section.

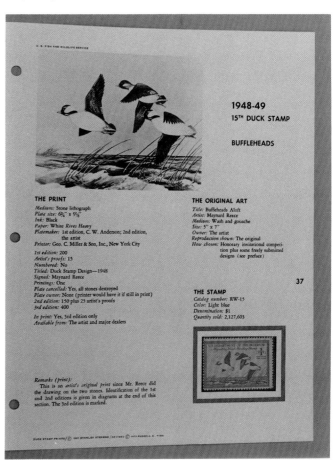

**1948-49**

**15TH DUCK STAMP**

**BUFFLEHEADS**

**THE PRINT**
*Medium:* Stone lithograph
*Plate size:* 6½" x 9½"
*Ink:* Black
*Paper:* White Rives Heavy
*Platemaker:* 1st edition, C. W. Anderson; 2nd edition, the artist
*Printer:* Geo. C. Miller & Son, Inc., New York City

*1st edition:* 200
*Artist's proofs:* 15
*Numbered:* No
*Titled:* Duck Stamp Design—1948
*Signed:* Maynard Reece
*Printings:* One
*Plate cancelled:* Yes, all stones destroyed
*Plate owner:* None (printer would have it if still in print)
*2nd edition:* 150 plus 25 artist's proofs
*3rd edition:* 400

*In print:* Yes, 3rd edition only
*Available from:* The artist and major dealers

**THE ORIGINAL ART**
*Title:* Buffleheads Aloft
*Artist:* Maynard Reece
*Medium:* Wash and gouache
*Size:* 5" x 7"
*Owner:* The artist
*Reproduction shown:* The original
*How chosen:* Honorary invitational competition plus some freely submitted designs (see preface)

37

**THE STAMP**
*Catalog number:* RW-15
*Color:* Light blue
*Denomination:* $1
*Quantity sold:* 2,127,603

**Remarks (print):**
    This is an *artist's* original print since Mr. Reece did the drawing on the two stones. Identification of the 1st and 2nd editions is given in diagrams at the end of this section. The 3rd edition is marked.

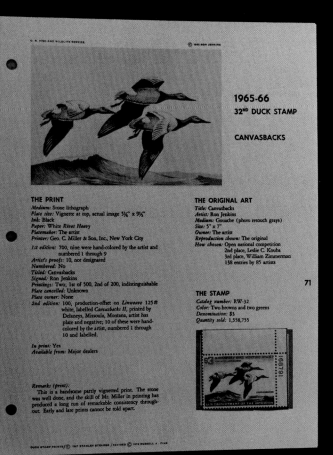

**1965-66**
32ND DUCK STAMP

**CANVASBACKS**

**THE PRINT**

*Medium:* Stone lithograph
*Plate size:* Vignette at top, actual image 5¾" x 9¼"
*Ink:* Black
*Paper:* White *River Heavy*
*Platemaker:* The artist
*Printer:* Geo. C. Miller & Son, Inc., New York City
*1st edition:* 700, nine were hand-colored by the artist and numbered 1 through 9
*Artist's proofs:* 10, not designated
*Numbered:* No
*Titled:* Canvasbacks
*Signed:* Ron Jenkins
*Printings:* Two; 1st of 500, 2nd of 200, indistinguishable
*Plate cancelled:* Unknown
*Plate owner:* None
*2nd edition:* 100, production-offset on *Linweave 125#* white, labelled *Canvasbacks II*, printed by Delaneys, Missoula, Montana, artist has plate and negative; 10 of these were hand-colored by the artist, numbered 1 through 10 and labelled.

*In print:* Yes
*Available from:* Major dealers

*Remarks (print):*
   This is a handsome partly vignetted print. The stone was well done, and the skill of Mr. Miller in printing has produced a long run of remarkable consistency throughout. Early and late prints cannot be told apart.

**THE ORIGINAL ART**

*Title:* Canvasbacks
*Artist:* Ron Jenkins
*Medium:* Gouache (photo retouch grays)
*Size:* 5" x 7"
*Owner:* The artist
*Reproduction shown:* The original
*How chosen:* Open national competition
   2nd place, Leslie C. Kouba
   3rd place, William Zimmerman
   138 entries by 85 artists

71

**THE STAMP**

*Catalog number:* RW-32
*Color:* Two browns and two greens
*Denomination:* $3
*Quantity sold:* 1,558,755

---

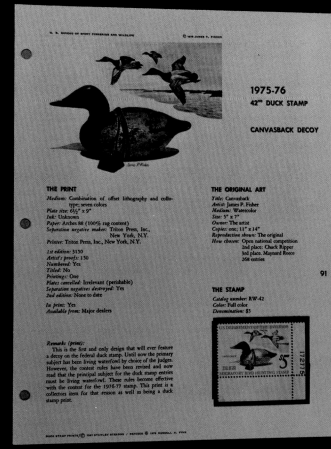

**1975-76**
42ND DUCK STAMP

**CANVASBACK DECOY**

**THE PRINT**

*Medium:* Combination of offset lithography and collo-type; seven colors
*Plate size:* 6½" x 9"
*Ink:* Unknown
*Paper:* Arches 88 (100% rag content)
*Separation negative maker:* Triton Press, Inc., New York, N.Y.
*Printer:* Triton Press, Inc., New York, N.Y.
*1st edition:* 3150
*Artist's proofs:* 150
*Numbered:* Yes
*Titled:* No
*Printings:* One
*Plates cancelled:* Irrelevant (perishable)
*Separation negatives destroyed:* Yes
*2nd edition:* None to date

*In print:* Yes
*Available from:* Major dealers

*Remarks (print):*
   This is the first and only design that will ever feature a decoy on the federal duck stamp. Until now the primary subject has been living waterfowl by choice of the judges. However, the contest rules have been revised and now read that the principal subject for the duck stamp entries must be living waterfowl. These rules become effective with the contest for the 1976-77 stamp. This print is a collectors item for that reason as well as being a duck stamp print.

**THE ORIGINAL ART**

*Title:* Canvasback
*Artist:* James P. Fisher
*Medium:* Watercolor
*Size:* 5" x 7"
*Owner:* The artist
*Copies:* one; 11" x 14"
*Reproduction shown:* The original
*How chosen:* Open national competition
   2nd place, Chuck Ripper
   3rd place, Maynard Reece
   268 entries

91

**THE STAMP**

*Catalog number:* RW-42
*Color:* Full color
*Denomination:* $5

---

*Canvasbacks* **
by Ron Jenkins, 1965-66

*Canvasback Decoy* **
by James P. Fisher, 1975-76

The first Pennsylvania
Waterfowl Management
Stamp **
by Ned Smith, 1983

# CHAPTER 15

*Accessories*

## CAST IRON ANIMAL FIGURES

Many animal figures were cast in iron as utilitarian or ornamental objects. Door stops, lawn sprinklers and garden ornaments were made by local foundries and some of them achieved national distribution. There are two series of lawn sprinklers, obviously made by the same foundries, but the writers have been unable to find any information on them. The Hubley Manufacturing Company of Lancaster, Pennsylvania made an extensive series of cast iron items, many in the shapes of birds and animals.

Frog iron doorstop **

Clay Pigeon iron doorstop ****

Pair of iron duck shaped doorstops **
Note duck on right called "Bashful"

Turtle iron doorstop **

Duck iron doorstop ***
a copy of an ATCO miniature

Alligator iron lawn sprinkler ***

Duck iron lawn sprinkler **

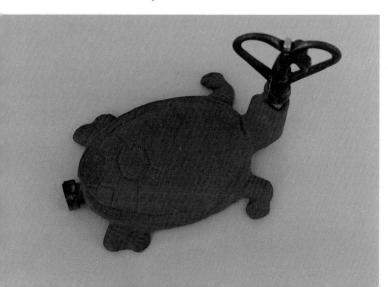

Duck iron lawn sprinkler ***
by Bradley & Hubbard Co.

Turtle iron lawn sprinkler **

**149**

Standing Frog iron lawn sprinkler ***
by NUYDEA

Wood Duck iron lawn sprinkler ***
by NUYDEA

NUYDEA logo appearing on the standing frog, wood
duck, and duck bird bath lawn sprinklers

Duck Bird Bath iron lawn sprinkler ★★★★
by NUYDEA

Frog iron lawn sprinkler ★★

151

## FISHING LURES AND EQUIPMENT

From the first hand-carved frog made by James Heddon in the 1890's to the multitude of lures made by later manufacturers, collectors prize these fish-enticers. Made from wood, metal, feathers, and thread, they encompass every conceivable idea that could lure fish. Some were probably made more for luring the angler than the fish.

The old wooden plugs came in many finishes from a covering of real frog skin through scale finishes to the standard red and white. The rarer finishes along with real glass eyes determine the collectability. The wooden store advertising plug and the duckling lure are also popular items in this field.

The fly rod lures made to imitate natural insects and aquatic life are highly desirable, especially if made by a well-known fly tier.

The tools needed by a well equipped angler including rods, reels, nets and creels round out the collecting possibilities.

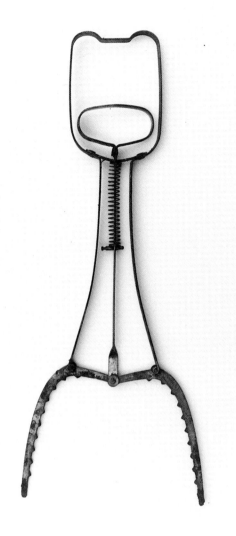

Marbles fish gaff **

Assorted fish gigs **

152

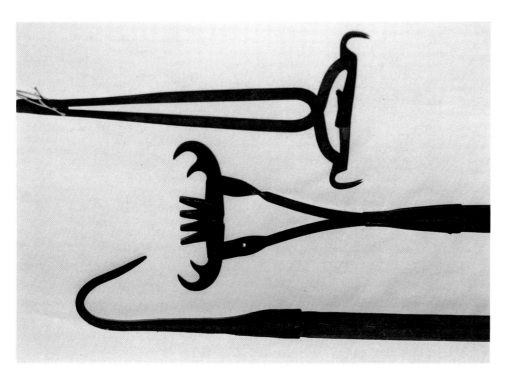

Fish gaffs **
The center gaff by Norlund of Williamsport, Pennsylvania

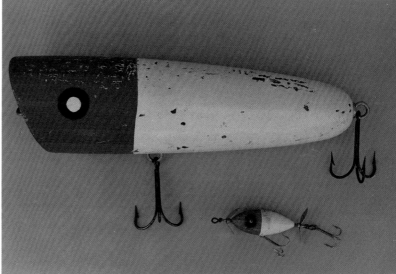

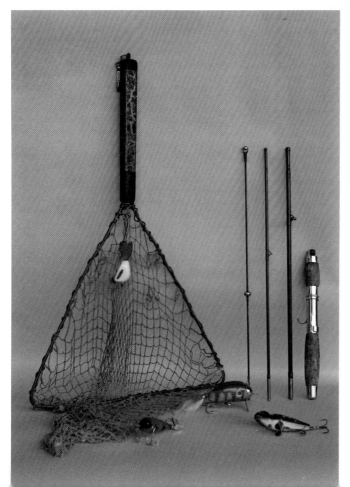

Large fishing lure store display **
26 by 12 inches, shown with a regular size plug for comparison

Triangular net and four-piece fishing rod **
a Coaxer shown on the net, ***
by W. J. Jamison Co., Chicago, Illinois
Red and black Dowagiac, Minnow Series O ***
by James Heddon & Sons, Dowagiac, Michigan
Redtail Automatic Striker ****
by Carl A. Johnson, Chicago, Illinois
Green jigger ***
by Creek Chub Bait Co., Garrett, Indiana *Jeff Rudy collection*

Fishing creel **
Jamison Frog Harness **
Frog Pappy, covered with real frog skin ***
by Eger Bait Mfg. Co., Bartow, Florida
Croaker, covered with real frog skin ***
by Paw Par Bait Co., Paw Paw, Michigan
James Hedden—wooden frog
made about 1898 ****
The first known rubber plug Pflueger frog ***
*Jeff Rudy Collection.*

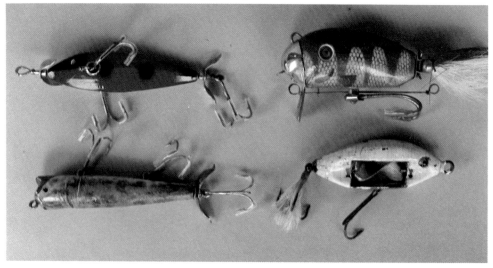

Red and black Dowagiac Minnow, Series O ***
Redtail Automatic Striker ****
Frog Pappy, covered with real frog skin ***
Chippewa Bass Bait ***
by Immell Bait Co., Blair, Wisconsin *Jeff Rudy collection*

Frog lures in a display case ***
*Jeff Rudy collection*

Duckling fishing lure **
by Bob White, Tullytown, Pennsylvania

Turtle and baby muskrat **
ice fishing lures

Ice fishing lure **

## GAME CALLS

As wildfowl became scarcer, larger numbers of decoys were needed and calling of the game became more of a necessity to get results. Imitations of duck and goose talk was tailored to regional requirements, just as various decoys were. Often, decoy carvers also made duck and goose calls. Wood was the usual material for these calls, but metal, hard rubber and other materials were also used. Early calls were utilitarian, but here and there makers showed artistic ability and produced beautiful works. Charles Perdew of Illinois was one of the best makers and his artistic calls are in great demand. As word of the success of these calls spread, other hunters made them to be used for different game. These, plus calls made in factories, form important parts of today's collections.

Pair of duck and goose calls **
carved by Mike Dieter, Manheim, Pennsylvania

Hardware store shot dispenser ***
"Dunscomb's Shot Case" patented July 15, 1878 by
Dillingham & Co., Sheboygan, Wisconsin

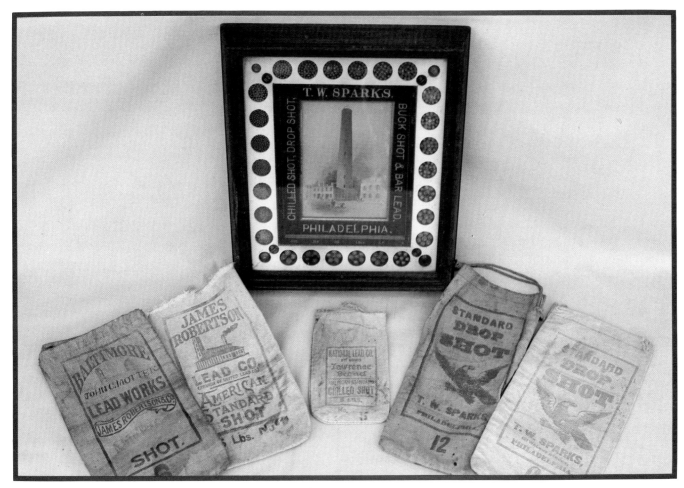

T. W. Sparks shot tower advertisement
and linen shot bags ***

## HARDWARE STORE ITEMS

Every small town had a hardware store and its items reflect the history of the area. For example, a counter-top shot dispenser "Dunscomb's shot case" held different size shot. By lifting the lever, the shot was dispensed.

The "Sparks deep frame" shows all the sizes of shot available and was a hand-designed and hand-lettered advertisement. The Sparks shot tower was located in Philadelphia.

Most sporting and hardware stores gave out yearly calendars with pictures by some of the best wildlife artists of the time.

# Bibliography

Brewster, Mel, *Remington Bullet Knives*, Collector Knives Press, Tacoma, Washington, 1991.

Coykendall, Ralf, Jr., *Coykendall's Sporting Collectibles Price Guide*, Lyons & Burford, New York, New York, 1991.

Dutton, William S., *Dupont, One Hundred and Forty Years*, Scribners, 1942.

Eaton, D.H., *Trapshooting, The Patriotic Sport* Sportsmens Review Pub. Co., Cincinnati, Ohio, 1920.

Fleckenstein, Henry A., Jr., *Decoys of the Mid-Atlantic Region*, Schiffer Publishing Ltd., West Chester, Pennsylvania, 1979.

Fleckenstein, Henry A., Jr., *American Factory Decoys*, Schiffer Publishing Ltd., West Chester, Pennsylvania, 1981.

Gerstell, Richard, *The Steel Trap in America*, Stackpole Books, Harrisburg, Pennsylvania, 1985.

Harlan, Howard Land, and Anderson, W. Crew, *Duck Calls*, Harlan Anderson Press, Nashville, Tennessee, 1988.

Iverson, Richard, *The Shotshell in the United States*, Circus Promotions, 1988.

Luckey, Carl F., *Old Fishing Lures and Tackle*, Books Americana, Inc., Florence, Alabama, 1986.

Lindsay, Ralph, *The Evolution of the Clay Pigeon*, The American Shotgunner, August, 1982.

Metz, Alice Huylett, *Early American Pattern Glass*, Spencer Walker Press, Columbus, Ohio, 1965.

Miller, Robert, *A Guide to Collecting Hunting and Fishing Licenses*, 1982.

# INDEX

**A**

Abbott, Jacob Bates, 103
Acme Folding Decoy Co., 31
Airtite Decoys, 29
Animal Trap Co., 35, 36, 37, 38, 53, 88, 90,
    117, 122, 148

**B**

Balsa King Decoy Co., 32
Barber, Joel, 100, 108, 110
Barnes, Sam, 18
Berg, Vic, 23
Bogardus Glass Target Ball Thrower, 80, 81
Bogardus, Adam H., 79, 80
Brass Shot Shells, 74, 75, 76
Brooks Co., 31

**C**

Canvas Decoy Co., 30
Card Glass Target Ball Thrower, 81
Carry-Lite Decoy Co., 54
Christmas Boxes, 66, 67, 68
Clifford, Robert, 44
Cobb, Nathan, 15
Cunningham, John, 42
Currier & Ives, 116
Currier, Jim, 18

**D**

Daisey, Delbert (Cigar), 15
Darling, J. N., 144
Decoys DeLux, 29
Decoys Unlimited, 43
Deiter, Mike, 156
Derrydale Press, 98
Deweys Owl & Crow Decoy, 32
Display of Collection, 7, 8
Dupe-a-goose, 27
DuPont, E. I. Co., 58, 72, 98, 111, 115,
    123, 124

**E**

Economy Powder Co., 59
Erwin, Robert, 21
Eveler, Walt, 21

**F**

Fibro-Lite Products Co., 30
Flap-o-matic Co., 28
Frost, A.B., 98, 111, 112

**G**

Gibbs, W.A., 92, 93, 94
Gipe, Ralph, 21
Glass Target Balls, 82, 83, 84
Goddard, Vincent, 23
Graham, Horace, 17
Grey, Zane, 98

**H**

Hancock, Miles, 47, 48, 49, 54
Handloading Process, 56, 57
Heddon, James & Sons, 153, 154
Heilner, Van Campen, 98
Herter Co., 27, 34, 48
Heverin, William, 17
Holland, Ray, 98
Hoosier Call Decoy Co., 3
Hudson, Ira, 13, 14
Hunt, Lynn Bogue, 98, 111, 113, 114, 115, 145
Hunter, Trader, Trapper Magazine, 95, 96

**J**

Jackson, Scott, 55
Johnson, William R. Co., 33
Joiner, Charles, 16, 17

**K**

K-D Decoy Co., 34
King's Powder Co., 58

**L**

Laflin & Rand Powder Co., 58, 72
Langford, Capt. Ike, 13
Lawson, Oliver, 40, 41, 42, 45, 53
Litzenberg, Bob, 19, 46

**M**

Marble Arms Co., 5, 91, 152
Martin Decoy Co., 38
Mason Decoy Co., 119
Mass & Steffen Fur Co., 96
McGaw, Bob, 50, 55
Megargee, Edwin, 111
Mitchell, Madison, 44
Montgomery Ward Co., 72, 73

**P**

Paper Shot Shells, 76, 77
Peters Cartridge Co., 8, 64, 67, 70, 71
Phillips, Edward J., 16
Pierce, Jim, 18, 19, 52
Powder Cans, 58, 59, 60
Pratt Decoy Co., 25
Pratt, Norris, 20
Preservation of Collection, 7, 8

**R**

Rarity, 9
Reed, James C., 14
Remington Arms Co., 61, 62, 63, 64, 71, 74,
    107, 118, 126, 127, 156
Remington Game Loads, 61, 62, 63, 64
Reynolds, J.W. Co., 31
Robin Hood Powder Co., 58, 65, 121
Rose Folding Decoy Co,, 30
Royal Bayreuth, 130, 131, 132, 133, 134
Rutledge, Archibald, 98

**S**

Seagram, Inc., 135
Selby Smelting & Lead Co., 70
Shertz, Paul, 116
Shot Shell Glasses, 136

Sinkbox Decoys, 20
Smith, Harry Worcester, 98
Smith, Ned, 146
South Bend Bait Co., 7
Sparks, T.W., 157
Sterling, J. Lloyd, 46, 47, 52
Strater & Sohier, 44

**T**

Traver, Capt. Josh, 16
Tyler, Lloyd, 49

**U**

U.S. Powder Co., 60
Union Metallic Cartridge Co., 65, 66, 67, 68, 74,
    75
United States Cartridge Co., 73, 107, 124, 125,
    126, 156
Urie, Jesse, 51

**V**

Value of Collection, 9
Victor Decoys, (see Animal Trap Co.)

**W**

Ward Brothers, 4, 10, 11, 12, 13, 40, 41, 50
Wasson Humane Trap, 94
Weiler, Milton, 4
Weller, Erwin Co., 7
West, Jim, 43
Western Cartridge Co., 70
White, Bob, 155
Wildfowler Decoy, 34, 35
Winchester Repeating Arms Co., 64, 65, 66, 70,
    75, 117
Window Shells, 77
Wolf, Joe, 104